STOP
PHYSICIAN
BURNOUT

What To Do When Working Harder Isn't Working

Dike Drummond, MD

To Gertrude Voris
Thank you for everything Granny.
I bet you didn't see this comin'.

CONTENTS

INTRODUCTION

"Be who you are and say what you feel,
for those who mind don't matter
and those who matter don't mind."
—Dr. Seuss

"Never mistake knowledge for wisdom.
One helps you make a living,
the other helps you make a life."
—Sandra Carey

WHAT YOU WILL FIND IN THIS BOOK

In 2011, I launched the website *TheHappyMD.com*. A few weeks later, I found myself talking with my first prospective burnout coaching client. "What's going on that has you talking to me today? Why did you reach out for support?" I asked him.

"I thought I was the most burned-out doctor in our group," Mike replied, his voice monotone. "Then, one of my partners killed himself last week. So, I thought I would give you a call."

We were both quiet for at least a full minute.

Unfortunately, I have heard this story many times since then. As physicians, we pride ourselves on the ability to work hard, soldier on, and keep going no matter what. This workaholic, "Lone Ranger" programming instilled over years of our medical education is one of the core causes of burnout, especially in men. This programming is so deep and wide we can suffer severe burnout for years, only jolted into taking action by the extreme circumstance of a partner's suicide.

My work with overstressed physicians—as well as the tools you will learn in this book—are inspired in large part by Mike's partner and others who lost their lives, careers, and marriages while under the influences of physician burnout. This crippling condition affects an average of one in three doctors on any given office day[1]. Tragi-

1

cally, Mike's partner couldn't see a way out of his downward spiral. We did not reach him in time.

However, his devastating action did have positive effects. It motivated Mike to seek help and he has recovered from his burnout after years of misery. His request for coaching in the early days of *TheHappyMD.com* allowed us to test the principles you will read in the pages ahead to ensure they work in the real world.

This book is my attempt to reach all physicians with the tools you need to understand, detect, prevent, and treat burnout. As we learn about our common enemy, it can bring us together to support each other more effectively and change physicians' workaholic, Lone Ranger, Superhero culture.

Mike was the first of hundreds of physicians who have allowed me to support their recovery to a more ideal practice and a more balanced life. We learned together what combination of tools would work to power his recovery.

This is one of the key learnings from my burnout work. Burnout is always multifactorial. It has multiple overlapping causes.

- Sometimes, a dozen smaller stresses gang up on you, setting up the classic "death by a thousand paper cuts."
- In other cases, you are stressed at work, but the final blow is when something happens at home—a parent becomes ill and moves in, or your spouse moves out.
- Or, a tragic event at work can add to the usual stress of a busy practice to push you over the edge.

Everyone's burnout is different. Recovery is a process of switching out old habits with new ones, one at a time.

A SYSTEMS APPROACH IS ESSENTIAL

That is what this book will teach you. You will see the systems of your life and career—and the overlap and interplay between them—in a new light. Like any ecosystem, changes in one system automatically affect the others. You can prevent burnout at work using actions you take at home. You can build more life balance with new actions you take at work.

In Mike's case, he was able to transition from a toxic workplace and severe burnout to a completely new position where he is happy, enjoys his practice again, and gets to spend more time with his family and riding his bike. He learned new tools to deal more effectively with stress at work. He built his Ideal Practice Description and used it for a focused job search. He learned how to make sure his weeks were more balanced than before. He learned how to take his life and career back and begin living on purpose. A series of small changes combined to stop his downward spiral and get him to a new place of satisfaction and fulfillment. You can use this book to do the same thing.

FIELD-TESTED, DOCTOR-APPROVED TOOLS

Since the day Mike and I met in 2011, I have delivered thousands of hours of one-on-one coaching to physicians—854 hours in 2013 alone. As I write this, we have 4,044 physicians subscribed to the newsletter at *TheHappyMD.com*, in sixty-three countries around the world. Our website and its library of free resources receives more than 10,000 visitors every month.

This ground level experience with doctors from all specialties has taught us what works with real doctors in real medical practices. I call the contents of this book "field-tested and doctor-approved" because it is true. They will work for you, too. With the tools in this book and the additional materials at our dedicated Resources Page at *TheHappyMD.com* website, you can accomplish any or all of the following:

1. Understand stress and burnout—most likely for the very first time.

There was no time to learn about burnout in medical school or residency. All the bandwidth was devoted to turning out a competent clinician. Unfortunately, the programming that puts us all at high-risk for burnout was instilled at the same time we were being molded into bright shiny young physicians.

And if that is not bad enough, I will wager you had several faculty members in your residency program who were the perfect example of the chronically overworked and burned-out physician. They modeled the burned-out doctor rather than the physician with a fulfilling practice and a well-balanced life.

This book will help you fill this gaping hole in your education once and for all. In chapter one, you will learn:

- Burnout symptoms and gender differences.
- Burnout causes, effects, and pathophysiology.
- How to recognize burnout in yourself and your colleagues.
- What I believe to be burnout's highest and best use.

2. Learn how to prevent and treat your own burnout.

We will not stop at the point of comprehension. Understanding is never enough to actually reap the rewards of a new concept. Understanding is the booby prize. Understanding changes nothing until you put it to use.

Unfortunately, most doctors have been trained by our decades in school to study a concept until we think we can answer a multiple-choice question on the topic. Typically, we study until we think we can pass the test. Then, we stop short of actually putting this new knowledge to use. Don't let this happen to you.

3. Build a more Ideal Practice and a more balanced life, no matter what.

If you are not suffering from burnout at the moment (though, perhaps you can see it coming if things don't change), I have good news. One of the fun things about these tools is they work for everyone, in every circumstance. They have unlimited upside.

You will learn to always be targeting and moving toward your Ideal Practice. If you are suffering from burnout, you will recover. If you are doing just fine, you will be able to build an even more Ideal Practice and balanced life.

You will learn to walk your personal path to a meaningful career and a fulfilling life with intention and purpose.

WHAT YOU WON'T FIND IN THIS BOOK

Untested theories and musing about things that *might* work.

Everything here is field-tested and doctor-approved—in *my* life and with hundreds of doctors in nearly every specialty and practice circumstance.

A literature review, lengthy bibliography, or complicated academic discussion.

Burnout is prevented by taking different actions. Everything here is keyed on giving you new awareness and teaching new actions for immediate results. I will give you selected references for key points along the way, but don't let your built-in bias toward needing to "review the literature" slow you down.

Try this instead. Learn a tool, and then put it to use in the testing ground of your own life. See if it works for you. Your life is your research laboratory. I promise I won't teach you anything that has not worked for at least a hundred doctors before you.

I will be continuously encouraging you to take action. Try things out in your life. Do something new in order to get new results. If it works, keep doing it. If it doesn't work, move on. This is exactly what you ask your patients to do. Now, it is your turn. Time for action, not further research.

<u>Complicated theories and named methodologies.</u>

Have you ever noticed that the rules to live a great life are very, very simple? We are taught the most complex concepts on the planet in our medical education, yet the principles of balance, happiness, and intention are all simple and easily understood. There is no rocket science here, but don't let that fool you.

- Clarity is power.
- Simplicity is power.
- More is not better.

Do not underestimate the ability of these straightforward tools and metaphors to help you take your life back, step by step. If you find yourself saying, "*It can't be that simple,*" then try it out and prove it to yourself. I dare you to pick just one tool, put it into action, and see what happens.

<u>Techniques that take a long time to pay off.</u>

I am just a simple country doctor. If a technique does not provide you with a benefit on the day you first put it into action, it is not in here. Many of these tools can be learned in five minutes, put into action tomorrow, and provide you with benefits before you go to bed that night. But don't take my word for it. Pick a tool and take action.

WHICH BRINGS US BACK TO MIKE, MY FIRST COACHING CLIENT

The principles gathered here are my attempt to ensure burnout never claims another victim like Mike's partner. These tools were handed to me by my own experience and tested by hundreds of our brothers and sisters who fought their way back into the light to rebound from burnout. I am thrilled to pass them on to you. Mike's partner has no idea of the contribution he has made to us all.

HOW TO GET THE MOST OUT OF THIS BOOK

"To exist is to change, to change is to mature,
to mature is to go on creating oneself endlessly."
—Henri Bergson

"The way to get good ideas is to get lots of ideas
and throw the bad ones away."
—Linus Pauling

Disclaimer 1—this book not just for physicians.

My work concentrates on physicians because I come from and operate in the world of doctors. They suffer a very high rate of burnout, making them an excellent group to study burnout symptoms, complications, and the tools for treatment and prevention.

At the same time, it is important to realize burnout affects all professions. No one is immune. Even though the burnout training that follows was developed by working with practicing doctors, it is applicable to—and appropriate for—anyone who is feeling stressed or burned-out by his or her job.

All who have direct patient contact as part of their usual job duties will benefit greatly from the discussion that follows: those within healthcare, physician's assistants, nurse practitioners, other nurses of all kinds—just substitute my use of the word *physician* or *doctor* with your own career title, and you will find this teaching completely relevant.

Disclaimer 2—this book is just as useful if you are NOT burned out.

You can use the training and tools that follow to create a more Ideal Practice and a more balanced life no matter how you feel about your practice at the moment. If you are doing well, you can use the very same burnout prevention skills below to do even better. After all, your choice to become a physician was meant to enable an extraordinary life. I will show you some field-tested ways to build that life, whether you are suffering from burnout or not.

FIVE KEYS TO ACCELERATE YOUR PROGRESS

1. Read this book…and do not stop there.

I will assume you bought this book for a reason. There is most likely something about your practice and your life you would like to change. For most people I meet, they look at the trajectory of their practice and don't like where things are headed. It is as if you have been on rails, like a train. You see where they started and where they are headed, and it is no longer what you want. You have probably been feeling this way for a while. You would really like to step off of this set of tracks.

If you want to learn more about the cause and cure of this dissatisfaction, you are in the right place.

Much of the change you seek is hidden in the programming we all acquired in our medical education. Burnout prevention depends on learning how to recognize this programming and the automatic habits it spawns and wake up. Lift your head, take charge, and start switching those habits out for living on purpose.

If you want to actually change your practice and your life, new awareness is mandatory and *not* sufficient all by itself. *Action* is the key.

I want to be very real with you here before we get started. Reading this book, if that is all you do, cannot help you make the changes you seek.

Consider Albert Einstein's definition of insanity:

> *"Insanity is doing the same things over and over*
> *and expecting a different result."*[2]
> —*Albert Einstein*

To get different results, *you must take different actions.*

Reading a book won't help until you use what you have learned to take different *actions* out in the real world.

This is why every section ends with ACTION STEPS. They are suggestions to put your new insights and these tools to use immediately. Each of the dozens of actions work individually; the key is to pick one and do it. This is the only way to step out of the Groundhog Day that is the insanity definition.

2. Journal.

Take notes as you read, preferably in a journal that is separate from the margins of this book. Though I love to write in the margins of good books, it limits you to short phrases of insight. There will be a number of times when the ideas below will have you journaling for several pages, if you are set up properly. Remember that insights are not action steps. You will have to go further than just a note or two in the margins if this book is to rise above the level of entertainment.

I encourage you to buy a nice journal and use it as a companion to this book.

At the end of each chapter, make sure you also journal on the ACTION STEPS. Use these to prompt your journal exploration of how these new levels of awareness and new burnout prevention tools would fit into and enrich your life.

Some of these passages will give words to things you have only experienced as feelings up until now. Write down your "ah-ha" moments and what new actions that "ah-ha" makes possible.

3. Overview and prioritize.

I encourage you to read a chapter at a time as an overview. Journal on the concepts and how they apply to your situation. Then, go back and dive a little deeper into the points that are most relevant to you.

Read through the first chapter on Burnout Basics, and make notes in your journal on the ways burnout works in your life and your practice. I have worked with hundreds of burned-out doctors, and I can assure you everyone's situation is unique. Your circumstances will not be a perfect match for any of your colleagues, although there are a small set of general themes.

Do not skip chapter 2 on Head Trash. You must identify and take out the trash first before the tools that follow can sink in. Notice what flavors of head trash are most common in your inner dialogue.

Chapter 3 holds the most important concepts in this entire book:

- Your Ideal Practice Description
- The Physician's Venn of Happiness
- Your Master Plan

Read through the chapter so you can see how these key concepts reinforce each other. Then, do create your version of all three. You will receive specific instructions on this process in the chapter.

Overview the entire tools section in chapter 4 so you can see the whole scope of what we will cover before you put any of the tools into action. Some will apply to your situation, and some will not. You get to pick favorites here. These are the building blocks for your own burnout prevention strategy.

4. Share your insights with colleagues, friends, and family.

I encourage you to share what you are learning—both in the book and about your-self—with physician colleagues, staff members, your significant other, and anyone else who could be a part of your support system going forward. My experience is that learning, growing, personal development, and self-exploration are radically accelerated when you are having conversations with people who care about you along the way.

Your connection could also prompt them to make some positive changes in their own lives.

If you really want to take this process to a new level of fun and speed, consider forming a study group. One structure that works is to read a chapter a week and journal on it. Bring your journal to a weekly meeting of your study group—either in-person or by phone or Skype—and share your insights and the action steps you will take in the week ahead.

You can become a mastermind group and mutual accountability buddies.

5. Use the Power Tools Library to go deeper and wider.

Please understand that this book is the tip of an iceberg of over 117 field-tested ways to lower your stress and prevent burnout. The Power Tools Library at *TheHappyMD.com* is packed with additional tools, videos, audio downloads, and even a free Discovery Session consult to give you a personal strategic plan.

A written book like this one can only appeal to one learning style. The additional Power Tools allow us to expand these teachings to all your senses and gives you access to a comprehensive library of tools to build your ideal practice.

See the last chapter on Next Steps for the full listing of nineteen additional Power Tools.

This is an exclusive FREE library of additional Ideal Practice building tools and training at the web address below:

www.thehappymd.com/powertools

All of these additional Power Tools are free and my gift to you as an owner of this book.

Most of all, get ready to look at what it means to be a physician in a whole new light. I want you to know there is no set of train tracks taking your career in a single, predetermined direction. The path you have been on is not set in stone. If you are ready to build your own Ideal Practice and start living on purpose, it is time to get started.

But before we do that, I'd like to share with you my own story of being burned to the ground twice and how it came to pass that you are reading this book now.

MY BURNOUT STORY (X2)

THE LESSONS I share in this book were ones I started learning as my own medical career came to a crashing halt in 1999, just after my fortieth birthday. It was a train wreck at the end of a multigenerational desire to have another doctor in the family.

THREE GENERATIONS TO DOCTOR NUMBER TWO

My great-grandfather was a GP during the Depression. My granny told stories about being paid in pies and chickens for her father's services. She and my mother each went to the University of Illinois wanting to become physicians. Somewhere along the way, they both diverted to a degree in education. Each had a long and rewarding career as a teacher.

When I, the first male grandchild, was born, these two powerful women focused their desire for another doctor in the family on me. By 1999, I had fulfilled their dream and became the quintessential small town family doctor, a real modern-day Marcus Welby type. I'd delivered over five hundred babies. I was chairman of the executive committee of our forty-doctor multispecialty group, as well as the managed care medical director back in the 1990s era of capitation. I had a young family and a turn of the century farmhouse on two acres in the country. I was living a dream we could trace back for three generations.

The Brick Wall of Burnout

Just after my fortieth birthday, everything came to a sudden and mysterious halt.

I can remember mind-numbing fatigue dropping over me like a blanket the instant I stepped into the office. It seemed like all joy and interest in my work, both as a clinician and a leader, drained away overnight. Food began to taste like sawdust. Color seemed to vanish from my surroundings—everything was black and white. In pictures from that time, I look like I was on chemotherapy.

I hoped that all I needed was a break from the routine. If I could just recharge my batteries, things would get better...right? I took a one-month sabbatical and did no work at all for the full thirty days. When I returned to my practice, I was only three hours into my first shift when I knew I could not continue. I put in my notice and walked away from my practice. I was at a dead end, nose against an immovable brick wall. I felt completely isolated, dazed, and confused.

Only one thing was clear: I was physically unable to keep going on this career path. My days as a full-time clinician were at an end.

The feeling of isolation was intense. No one reached out to me. There were no resources on burnout at the time. Google wasn't founded until 1998. Imagine that for just a second—I actually didn't figure out I was suffering from career-ending burnout until a couple of years later.

This would turn out to be the first of two times I have been burned to the ground. In this case, the career I gave to my twenties was gone. I never doubted things would be okay and I would find another way to make a living, but I walked away without a transition plan. I do not recommend repeating my mistake. If this feels familiar to you, I have just one piece of advice: do not quit without a transition plan and a clear understanding of what you really want going forward.

I made the classic physician mistake of being completely focused on avoiding what I didn't want. I was running away from what my career had become. I was not running toward anything. I had no idea what I really wanted. My only clarity was what I didn't want and couldn't continue doing.

In the years from 2000–2005, I put food on the table working locum tenens as an urgent care physician. It was a soul-sucking exercise in suffering for me. Nothing made me want to be there, except for the handful of patients each day who I liked and enjoyed.

The Birth of an Entrepreneur

Around that same time, my wife started a training company. Together, we built it into a very successful small business, teaching leadership and meeting facilitation skills to the US Navy's LEAN/Six Sigma Black Belt Certification Program. As the COO, I learned the Internet from the ground up—blogging, website development, and how to get on the first page of Google. I became a certified professional coach and have coached entrepreneurs and physicians since 2001. By 2005, we were successful enough that I was able to stop my locum tenens work. I have not seen patients in a clinical setting since then.

I had made a successful transition from practicing physician to entrepreneur. We were making more money than I had ever taken home as a physician. I was able to put my children on the bus in the morning and make them snacks when they got off again in the afternoon. I was living the entrepreneur dream many physicians yearn for on a difficult practice day. Unfortunately, it didn't last.

Round Two

In 2010, my twenty-four year marriage ended, and I was burned to the ground for a second time.

I was on my own for the first time since my children had been born. I had nothing left to lose, so I decided to focus all my efforts on a dream I had held onto for a decade—building a coaching business to help doctors facing their own brick wall of burnout. I knew there were physicians out there in situations similar to what I went through in 1999. I could feel their pain like a band of pressure across my shoulder blades as I researched ways to help them in this new Internet-driven world. I felt called to action by the size of the need and my own personal experience of what they were going through.

Burnout is worse now than in the 1990s. I wondered if there was someone visible they could turn to for help. So, I did what any physician would do in 2010 and Googled "physician burnout." The results were either depressing or dangerous, depending on the mental state of the person looking at the first page.

It was nothing but prevalence studies.

Now, if I am burned out to the point of contemplating suicide, there is nothing more depressing than a series of prevalence studies. I don't need to learn how common burnout is; I want a way out, a cure, something, *anything* to feel better. Google was no use here. Fortunately, my entrepreneur experience taught me how to get on the first page of Google. It was time to push the prevalence links out of the way and give visitors proven tools to feel better right away. It was time to give them something they could actually use.

Step two was a literature review—a pretty standard move for a physician, after all. I was surprised again by what I found. There were dozens of studies showing what works to lower physician stress and prevent burnout. There was also a consistent co-incidence: every single one of the tools research had proved effective were things I had either already incorporated into my own life, taught my coaching clients, or both. These tools included things like mindfulness, meditation, journaling, exercise, yoga, work-flow tools, strategic planning, communication, emotional intelligence tools, and life-scheduling techniques. I was living, breathing, and coaching them all.

I was Being Prepared to Share a Cup of Coffee

In years past, I have often asked myself in a semi-joking fashion, *I wonder what I will do when I grow up?* Here is where that question was answered for me. Since that day in 2010, I have been all grown up. I know the work I will be doing until I can no longer work. It came to me like the light on the road to Damascus, sudden and certain.

I knew in my heart that my medical career didn't have to end in 1999. If I had just been able to have a cup of coffee with someone who could tell me what it was that I was experiencing and who could give me some tools to change without having to walk away, that conversation would have completely altered the trajectory of my life.

I realized in a flash that my journey had specifically prepared me to be the person I would have wanted to have that cup of coffee with back in 1999. The 2010 version of me could have showed my 1999 self so many ways forward. The only logical explanation I could reach was that I was being prepared to teach other physicians how to prevent and recover from burnout. I tested this hypothesis immediately.

The Birth of *TheHappyMD.com*

I put up a bare bones website at a URL that made sense to me: ***TheHappyMD.com***, the place to find "The Tools So YOU Can Be a Happy MD."

I wrote my original article, "Physician Burnout—Why It's Not a Fair Fight," and put it up on my website. I pitched it to Kevin Pho, MD, at his very popular website ***www.KevinMD.com***. I created a free report called the *Satisfaction Mind Flip* and made it available for download at my website.

Kevin published that article. Doctors began streaming to the website and downloading the report. Everyone who comes to the site is offered a free "Discovery Session." This is a one-hour phone call, a virtual "cup of coffee," if you will, so I can make sure they don't walk away from their career like I did.

We Have Never Looked Back

The *Satisfaction Mind Flip* has been joined by other free reports, including the *Burnout Prevention Video Training Series* and the *MATRIX Report* with over 117 ways to prevent burnout. Everything we teach is simple to implement and produces immediate results. Anyone who books a Discovery Session walks away with a strategic plan to move forward without walking away from their career, unless walking away is the healthiest option. If a job change is necessary, we have discovered a whole new method to find a good match for your Ideal Practice in the transition.

I am overjoyed to find my purpose and a right livelihood in what felt for so long were the ashes of my career as a doctor. It is clear that burnout is directly linked to quality, safety, patient satisfaction, group culture, and the ability to adapt and innovate in our rapidly changing healthcare industry. We are blessed to be making a huge impact addressing a universal need among today's physicians. At this point, all my "patients" are doctors. This book is my effort to share with you many of the things I have learned in my own burnout journey and from hundreds of our sisters and brothers in the frontlines of patient care.

My intention is to show you how to prevent burnout and much more. When you use these same tools proactively, they will allow you to build an amazing life around your Ideal Practice. I am so glad you are here. I can't wait to show you what is possible for you and your family.

CHAPTER 1

BURNOUT BASICS

Everything You Need to Understand About Burnout, but Didn't Know to Ask

"It is difficult to get a man to understand something when his salary depends upon his not understanding it."
—Upton Sinclair

"If you have always done it that way, it's probably wrong."
—Charles Kettering

WHY IS BURNOUT SUCH A BIG DEAL FOR DOCTORS?

Burnout is more common in physicians than other professions.[3]

In healthcare, the effects of burnout have negative—and potentially fatal—repercussions for a huge swath of society. In no other occupation does burnout exact such a toll of waste, morbidity, and mortality.

<u>Physician burnout has been linked to:</u> [4]

- Lower care quality
- Lower patient satisfaction rates
- Higher medical error rates
- Higher malpractice risk
- More frequent disruptive physician behavior
- Higher turnover in physicians and staff members (nothing turns over your staff better than working with a burned-out doctor)
- Higher rates of physician divorce
- Physician alcohol and drug use and addiction
- Suicide

The bottom line is this: physician burnout sends out huge ripples of pervasively negative effects in all directions.

Burnout is bad:

- For the doctor
- For their family
- For their patients
- For their staff, colleagues, and co-workers
- For their organization

But wait, there's more …

Burnout is everywhere, all the time.

BURNOUT PREVALENCE

The prevalence of symptomatic burnout is staggeringly high in practicing physicians. Consider the following quote from one of the main researchers on burnout prevalence from a JAMA article several years back:

"Numerous global studies involving nearly every medical and surgical specialty indicate that approximately 1 of every 3 physicians is experiencing burnout at any given time."[5]

In fact, the prevalence of burnout is the single most thoroughly studied aspect of this issue. No population has endured more burnout surveys than physicians. The statistics are stable over decades, across specialties, and between nations.

Whether you are looking at Japanese ENTs, Irish OB/GYNs, family doctors in the US, or anesthesiologists in Australia, an average of 1 in 3 physicians are suffering from symptomatic burnout on any given office day.

As this book goes to press, the acceleration of change in the US healthcare market with the Affordable Care Act and the wave of consolidations it is driving appear to be causing burnout prevalence to reach new highs in many organizations.

And yet, most healthcare workplaces completely fail to acknowledge stress, burnout, and overwhelm. The physicians and staff are running on their gerbil wheels as fast as they can. You might finish seeing patients at five, work on your charts until seven, drag yourself home for dinner, and put in two more hours on the charts at home only to stagger back into an identical day tomorrow. Sound familiar? It is certainly common. That, however, is not the worst part.

LEADERSHIP CAPITULATION IS THE BIGGER TRAGEDY

In many organizations, the leadership has thrown in the towel. They have given up on the possibility of things being different. They have resigned themselves—and, by proxy, all of their employee physicians—to burnout being a normal and inevitable component of a modern physician's life. In my experience, only 10-15 percent of organizations care enough about the doctors in the frontline to do anything proactive to prevent burnout. The vast majority of organizations have given up caring about the people providing the patient care. They simply hire more doctors to cover the turnover as physicians burn out or move on.

I find this fascinating, given the nature of services we provide in healthcare. We care for others. Our caring is the basis of the business of healthcare. Our caring is what puts dollars in the organization's coffers and supplies the income that is the business's lifeblood. But who is caring for the doctors?

A LESSON FROM EVERY OTHER INDUSTRY

Look at any industry outside of healthcare, and listen to what the acknowledged leaders say about their people. Inevitably a reporter gets around to asking, "To what do you attribute your company's success?"

The leader will then say something like, "It's simple really. We hire the best people we can find and take really good care of them."

Why does healthcare not follow this rule?

If you find yourself in a hostile workplace where no one seems to understand or care about your personal health or your workplace conditions, I invite you to dive into this book and learn how to look out for yourself. You will learn a number of ways to improve your current situation and how to conduct a high quality job search if it is healthier for you to move on.

If you find yourself in a forward-thinking organization that cares about you and works to provide the support you need to do a good job with your patients, congratulations. It is highly likely they gave you this book. You can use the following tools to focus squarely on creating your Ideal Practice.

Always remember, burnout is not normal or inevitable.

Even though burnout is common, it is not normal. Burnout is identifiable, preventable, and treatable. Burnout even has its benefits for you personally and for the forward-thinking healthcare organization.

You can use your own stress and burnout to create a more Ideal Practice and a more balanced life—much more quickly than you might imagine.

If you are a leader in a healthcare organization, we are entering healthcare's "Age of Engagement." From this point forward, your proactive efforts to lower stress and create a more physician-friendly workplace will give you a massive competitive advantage over all other organizations that just keep piling it on the docs.

WHAT IS THE DIFFERENCE BETWEEN BURNOUT AND NORMAL STRESS?

STRESS IS COMMON. It's a normal aspect of modern life. It's nearly constant for a physician on the job. With stress an ever-present condition for every practicing doctor, how can you tell the difference between the "normal" stress of practicing medicine and burnout?

Before we get to that simple answer, let's remember that stress is not always a bad thing. Without an appropriate amount of stress and challenge, the average human lapses into boredom and inactivity. The stress and responsibility of caring for patients is part of the motivation to do your best in every case. The perfectionism it inspires is a good thing for the patient. However, too much of that good thing is bad for the doctor.

So, what is the difference between the normal stresses of the healthcare workplace and the syndrome of burnout? It's really important that you and I get on the same page here in regards to this critical distinction.

Burnout is not about what is happening to you.

The difference between burnout and normal stress is not the nature of the external events that you find stressful. What one person finds to be stressful, a different person would experience as stimulating, exciting, and even fun. Everyone's situation is unique.

Burnout is about whether or not you can cope with the things you find stressful.

The difference between simple stress and burnout is your ability to respond to and recover from the energy drain caused by the things that stress you out.

With normal stress …

… You are able to recover with time off. You are able to maintain "energetic homeostasis." You can recover your energy, enthusiasm, and drive with adequate rest. Your energy may be higher some days and lower on others. You notice the day-to-day fluctuation in your energy levels; however, you don't feel overwhelmed or incapable of recovery from week-to-week.

With burnout …

…You are unable to recover. Your energy enters the pattern of a relentless downward spiral. There comes a time when you notice you are not bouncing back, and you dread heading back into work. In most cases, a person suffering from burnout will eventually say something like, "I'm not sure how much longer I can go on like this."

The only reason burnout rates can hover in the 30 percent range for decades and not destroy the practice of medicine is because we've been work-hardened to tolerate this energetic drain. Let's face it—our training is a gladiator-style survival contest. We are conditioned to be able to cope with burnout better than all but a handful of other service-oriented professions—law enforcement and active duty military come immediately to mind. We will talk much more about this below when we discuss the pathophysiology of burnout.

This high level overview will make one thing obvious. If you are burned out or headed in that direction, there is something about the stress at work and the things you do now to recover that are not working. You are leaking energy and not replenishing it, like a boat with a hole so large that bailing as fast as you can does not keep you from sinking.

This is why a sabbatical will never cure burnout. It provides only temporary relief. When you return to the workplace and your normal life after your sabbatical, the excess drain begins anew. You will be right back here in short order. There is still a hole in your boat.

MEASURING BURNOUT—THE GOLD STANDARD

IN THE 1970S, a researcher at the University of San Francisco named Christina Maslach, along with her partners Susan Jackson and Michael Leiter, constructed what has become the gold standard in measuring occupational burnout. The twenty-two question survey is known as the Maslach Burnout Inventory (MBI).

The MBI measures the severity of the three main symptoms of burnout:

1. Exhaustion

You are extremely tired and unable to recover. Things are either chronically miserable or on the downward spiral trajectory.

2. Depersonalization

This is an unfeeling or impersonal attitude toward the people you are meant to serve. You will recognize this as the common healthcare symptom of "compassion fatigue."

The doctor becomes cynical or sarcastic about his or her patients. They may blame the patient for contributing to their own personal stress levels. In some cases, the physician may have fantasies about getting rid of certain patients in creative ways such as throwing them out the window or even more bizarre and violent visions.

In some healthcare work environments, depersonalization, sarcasm, and cynicism are constant and pervasive. Individuals will continuously blame and complain about patients in the break room and try to normalize it by calling it "healthy venting." Remember this: compassion fatigue is a symptom of burnout. Being cynical and sarcastic about your patients is not normal, and it is never healthy.

On a deeper level, compassion fatigue is actually a dysfunctional psychological defense mechanism. When you are burned out, the cynicism and sarcasm creates a psychological barrier between you and your patient—the source of your energy drain.

However, compassion fatigue only accelerates your downward spiral, because it violates one of healthcare's prime directives: *The patient comes first.* You feel a few seconds of release from bad-mouthing a non-compliant patient at the cost of feeling much worse shortly thereafter.

3. Lack of Efficacy

This symptom manifests when you begin to doubt the purpose of the work that you do. A physician at this stage will say something like, "What's the use? I don't know why I keep going. My work isn't really helping anybody or serving any purpose."

Other physicians will begin to doubt the quality of their work or worry about making a clinical mistake because of their exhaustion and obvious compassion fatigue.

Put them all together and the full MBI expression of burnout includes:

- Exhaustion
- Cynicism, sarcasm, and compassion fatigue
- "What's the use?"

In the years since Christina Maslach and her colleagues constructed the MBI, it has become the most widely used inventory for detecting burnout and measuring its severity in healthcare, education, human services, and many other industries.

GENDER DIFFERENCES IN BURNOUT SYMPTOMS

As more and more female physicians have entered the workforce, recent data is providing confirmation that there are gender differences in burnout symptoms. Think about this for a moment. I am certain you know some burned out doctors. In your mind's eye, put the women on one side and the men on the other. What differences in their behavior do you notice?

Here is what a recent paper is showing[6]. I bet it backs up your personal observations.

Female Pattern Burnout

On average, women physicians experience burnout symptoms in the same order as Christina Maslach originally documented them:

1. Exhaustion
2. Cynicism, sarcasm, compassion fatigue
3. "What's the use?"

Male Pattern Burnout

On average, male burnout follows this pattern:

1. Cynicism, sarcasm, and compassion fatigue
2. Exhaustion

3. "What's the use?" goes completely missing. It is rare for a male physician to doubt the meaning or quality of his work.

This leads to the common stereotype of the male doctor in his 50s, chronically burned out, viciously cynical, often disruptive, who continues to soldier on and tells himself, "I am still doing good work."

One More Gender Difference

Here is one more gender difference I have noticed from working with hundreds of burned out doctors: once a woman reaches a certain point in her downward spiral, she will usually confide in someone or ask for help.

Most men do not.

I am often asked why this is the case. I think the explanation is simple and based on differences in neuroanatomy and conditioning between the sexes.

Women tend to discuss emotions. They tend to have female friends they confide in. They find it more difficult to tolerate the emotional toll of the battle between compassion fatigue and "the patient comes first."

Men don't ask directions when lost behind the wheel of a car. They don't ask for help when their career is in jeopardy either. We have fewer close friends and tend not to talk about emotional issues. In the competitive world of the average man, admitting distress is synonymous with weakness or failure. For many men, reaching out for help—or admitting you can't keep going on like this—is a final act of capitulation and surrender that takes place long after the average woman has already admitted her burnout to someone else.

How This Shows Up in My Coaching Practice

My website at *TheHappyMD.com* receives 10,000 site visits a month. I believe the proportion of women and men in the general physician population is about 50:50 at this point. However, amongst the physicians who actually ask me for help by becoming a coaching client, 85 percent are women.

WHAT IS THE PATHOPHYSIOLOGY OF BURNOUT?

REMEMBER PATHOPHYSIOLOGY? THE classes we could only take after learning the normal physiology of the various organ systems? It covers all the different ways infections and diseases do the damage that they do. Cancers can hide from the immune system. Cholera turns our intestinal absorption system inside out to do its dirty work. So what, then, might be the pathophysiology of burnout?

Just how does it take the smartest, hardest-working people on the planet and drag them slowly to their knees? Before I show you the three-part answer to that question, let's get rid of a metaphor that simply doesn't reflect reality: *My batteries just need recharging.*

It is Not About Your Batteries

Imagine the Energizer Bunny™. He is marching along, beating his little drum.

What happens to the rabbit when his battery runs out? He stops dead in his tracks. He cannot walk or beat that drum until you install a new battery.

The difference between a battery-powered toy bunny and a physician is simple: you have never, ever stopped working. You have a personal experience of working far past the point of your batteries being completely dead. You were trained to keep working on empty and below. You never stop. Never.

The battery metaphor for the energy of a physician is inaccurate. Here is a better one.

Your Energetic Bank Accounts

Think about an energetic bank account. It is just like your checking account, except instead of money, it holds your personal store of energy. It might look like this:

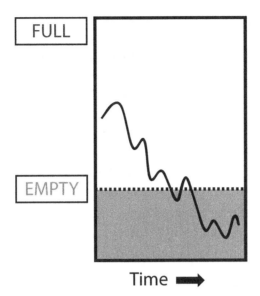

Notice that this energy account has a full mark and an empty mark, but it does not stop at empty. Like most bank accounts, it can fall to a negative balance. You can be below zero and the account still exists.

What happens if you overdraw your checking account? Does the bank close it? Nope. They simply charge you fees and interest and you go even further into the red. When you cross zero, it simply accelerates the downward spiral.

It is exactly the same for your energy. When you cross the empty boundary, the downward spiral often accelerates. However, you do not stop showing up for work and seeing patients, at least not for a while.

Here's why: your residency was a specific work-hardening process. You were trained to function as a doctor when your energy account was tapped dry. You have been conditioned to run on empty and below.

Studies show you are not at your best when your energy levels are below zero. Your quality of care and patient satisfaction scores will suffer. Despite that, you will still get the work done somehow, finish your shift, and drag your sorry butt home…right?

Here's the problem. The only way you can do your best work with patients and the only way you can have any reasonable quality of life at home is to somehow maintain a positive balance in your energy account. This brings us to the First Law of Burnout.

THE FIRST LAW OF BURNOUT

"You Can't Give What You Ain't Got"

Without a positive balance of personal energy, you have nothing to give. If you continue to put out energy when you are below zero, the care you offer and the life you live will be a shadow of what is possible for you.

Let's go one step further.

Your three energy accounts

Let's add in another very useful distinction here. For my coaching clients and me, it very useful to think in terms of three distinct energy accounts. These accounts correspond to each of the three symptoms of the Maslach Burnout Inventory (MBI).

Let me show you each of these three energy accounts in turn and give you a recipe for keeping each of the three accounts in a positive balance.

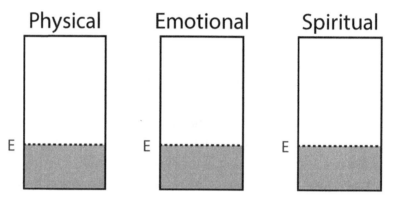

1. Exhaustion and Your Physical Energy Account

The MBI symptom of exhaustion corresponds to an account holding your physical energy. This is a simple enough concept. We are human beings with a physical body to which we must tend. You keep this account full by taking good care of your physical self.

This is another area where our training taught us exactly the opposite. Long shifts, poor nutrition, no exercise, and sleep deprivation are all part of the work-hardening of residency. If you learned how to take good care of yourself, it was not while you were at work.

Each of us must plan and execute a physical care program to keep ourselves healthy. Rest, good food, exercise, and adequate time off for recharge are all important. This is your personal responsibility, no matter what practice structure (from solo to employee) or job situation you find yourself in at the moment.

2. Compassion Fatigue and Your Emotional Energy Account

The MBI symptom of cynicism, sarcasm, and compassion fatigue corresponds to an account holding your emotional energy. Remember, "You can't give what you ain't got." If you are not getting your emotional needs met and this account is in a negative balance, you cannot be emotionally present for the pain and suffering of others. This is where compassion fatigue flies in as a defense mechanism and tries to help out. Unfortunately, it only makes things worse.

You fill this energy account by having adequate time for the important relationships in your life. Are you spending enough time with the people you love? Or, can you think of a number of people you really would like to spend more time with and it just never seems to happen? For most practicing physicians, there is a huge imbalance between the time you spend at work—or after work on work activities—and the time you would like to spend with your children, friends, significant other, and family. How about you?

3. "What's the use?" and Your Spiritual Energy Account

I want to separate the concept of spirituality I am referencing here from any type of religious practice. If you have a religious practice that comforts you, please keep it up. When I use the word *spirituality*, I am talking about your week-to-week connection with a sense of purpose and meaning in your work and your life.

In an ideal world, your medical practice would provide you with that sense of purpose and fulfillment early and often. You would have frequent patient interactions where, at the end of the day, you look back and say to yourself, "Oh, yeah, *that* is why I became a doctor!"

This is not to say you must derive your entire sense of purpose from your medical practice. Many of us find purpose in family activities and other interests outside of medicine. What provides you will that deep down "oh, yeah" feeling?

You make a deposit into your spiritual energy account whenever you feel that connection between what you are doing and your purpose, when what you are doing feels like *what you are meant to be doing* in this lifetime. You are making the difference you were put here to make with the people you are meant to help.

How—specifically—can you make deposits in your spiritual energy account?

That depends on where you derive your sense of purpose. If we focus only on your medical practice for a moment, let me show you a way to get started.

Grab a piece of paper and a pen. Go on, do it. It does you no good whatsoever to simply read about this exercise.

Write down, in as much detail as you can, your last meaningful patient encounter. Write down that last patient visit where you said, "Oh, yeah, that's why I do what I do," or where you came home that evening and shouted out as you walked through the door, "Honey, honey …sit down for a minute and let me tell you what happened at work today."

Write it down now with all the details you can muster.

- What happened?
- How did it feel?
- Why did it feel that way?

When you are done, read it back to yourself.

- What are the themes you see in this story?
- Is this a particular type of patient or diagnosis or procedure you really like?
- Was it more about the problem or more about your relationship with the patient?
- What else was special about this particular encounter?

And here is the payoff question: *How can you structure your day so this kind of encounter is more frequent?*

Setting yourself up to have more frequent ideal patient encounters is an important part of building your Ideal Practice. You can structure your weeks to increase the likelihood of this kind of interaction.

Your Spiritual Energy Account and the Triple Whammy

Here is a special attribute I have noticed about this third energy account. Check it out and see if this is true for you.

Whenever you have a patient encounter that gives you that sense of purpose and fulfillment—as you feel it make a deposit in your spiritual bank account—you can feel the other two energy accounts go up at the same time.

One experience of being connected with your purpose gives you an energy deposit in all three accounts. It is a true triple whammy.

Remember, too, that this same connection with your purpose could come from outside your medical practice. You could get the same triple deposit from coaching your children's soccer team, volunteering to teach kids to read, overseas medical missions, or anything else that feeds your spirit. You can structure your life to increase the frequency of these experiences, too.

It is part of stepping off those rails and living with purpose.

Unfortunately, we tend to lose sight of purpose when we are overwhelmed and exhausted. Maintaining your ability to focus on what you love about your practice—and your sense of purpose in what you do—is one of the lessons I hope you take from this book.

Burnout pathophysiology ACTION STEPS

Using the diagrams below, place an "X" where you feel your energy balances are for your three energy accounts at the moment.

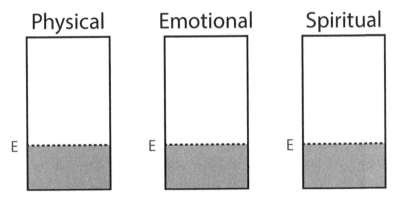

Just becoming aware of your balances in these energy accounts is a huge change for most doctors. Remember, our "patient comes first" training taught us how to completely ignore these energetic signals. It is high time for you to develop the ability to monitor your own energy stores.

Keep in mind: *You can't give what you ain't got.*

WHAT CAUSES BURNOUT?

WHEN I FIRST started coaching physicians, I thought this question had a simple answer. I thought of it like a third grade math equation.

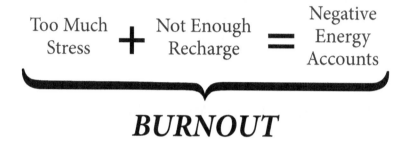

Too much stress on the job and not enough recharge off the job caused a negative energy balance. This situation is the very definition of burnout.

Since then, I have learned the sources of stress and the blockages to recharge are much more complicated than simple third grade math. Otherwise, why would one third of our best and brightest be stuck in burnout every day? It is a conundrum for sure.

By the time I was working with my fiftieth burnout coaching client, several distinct patterns had emerged. I had stumbled onto what I believe are the four main causes of burnout. That's right, four distinct and separate causes of the energy drain that leads to burnout. Some of them are indeed stress-related. Others are the result of blind spots instilled by the conditioning (or, you could say, brainwashing) process of our medical education.

Let's go through each one. I encourage you to notice that your training only prepared you for one of these four main causes of burnout. No wonder burnout is capable of sneaking up on so many of us.

THE FOUR ROOT CAUSES OF BURNOUT

Burnout Cause #1: The Practice of Medicine

By any measure, the practice of medicine is stressful. Apart from law enforcement and active-duty military (two careers that also have very high burnout rates), medicine may be the most stressful career you could choose.

You have ultimate responsibility and little control over the outcome, but that is not all. The following story will illustrate a little-appreciated stress of being a doctor that all of us notice in our training when we first start seeing live patients. It doesn't take long, though, for this source of stress to fall into a deep blind spot in our awareness. Talking about this stress to doctors is very much like talking to a fish about the water in their bowl. The fish is constantly steeped in and completely unaware of the water.

Everyone who is not a doctor sees this stress of working as a physician immediately. It becomes invisible for doctors early in our training because it is part of the fabric of every single patient encounter.

The Restaurateur vs. The Physician

I have a friend who is a restaurateur. He owns a combination sushi bar and Japanese steak house. In the front of the restaurant, the little plates of sushi float by your seat like boats on a river. In the back, they slice and toss your food on a hot burner in the middle of the table and make the onion volcano. You know the one.

That is how my friend makes a living. Every time I see him, he is smiling. One night, I asked him what it's like to have this for a job.

He said, "Dike, I love my job. Everyone comes in here determined to have a good time. My job is just to not screw that up for them."

Think about that for a second. How is being a physician different than owning a Japanese steak house—or almost any other job?

No one wants to come and see you …ever.

They don't expect to have a good time during their visit to the doctor under any circumstances. Even a routine physical is filled with trepidation. Who knows what you might find out?

Even if you are not the patient, you don't want to visit your family in the hospital or accompany them on their visit. Who knows what the doctor might find and what it might mean?

Our "clients" are sick, hurting, injured, scared, and sometimes in the very act of dying. Every visit is veiled by a mist of these negative emotions. You can't escape this reality. It quickly fades from our awareness. It never actually goes away.

For all the reasons mentioned above, and many more you will learn in the pages that follow, the modern practice of clinical medicine is stressful.

Even if I could magically shift you from room to room in a Star Trek-like transporter beam and relieve you of all documentation requirements (wouldn't that be nice!), allowing you the classic physician's dream experience of "just seeing patients" would still leave you drained by the activities of your day.

And then there are the bad days.

No one can make it through training and into private practice without being traumatized by horrific events along the way. We all have stories we have never told anyone. We have all seen things happen we wish we hadn't. It goes with the territory. Each of us has one or more traumatic experiences from our past that is capable of blowing a "normal" day to pieces when circumstances align themselves to remind us of the original incident.

Each of us also knows that every patient could be the next missed diagnosis or allergic reaction.

This work is stressful in so many ways.

The Energetic Reality

From the standpoint of your energy accounts, you cannot work in the office and/or hospital without expending physical, emotional, and spiritual energy. You will come home with less energy than when you arrived at the beginning of your shift.

...And the Exception

The one exception is if you had a major ideal patient encounter that day and created your own triple whammy energy deposit. For most physicians, these types of encounters are rare and their practice is not designed to deliver them with any frequency.

It is very important to note that this is the only burnout cause you had any experience with when you graduated from residency. You will soon see you are completely unprepared for the remaining three burnout causes. Hang on to your hat.

Burnout Cause #2: Your Specific Job

The second root cause of burnout is the stress associated with *your specific job position*. These stresses are deposited in an additional layer on top of the level one stresses of the practice of clinical medicine outlined above.

A very incomplete list of job-specific stresses includes:

- Your scheduling template and patient volume requirements
- The Electronic Medical Record in your institution, the IT capabilities that support your EMR, and your specific documentation requirements—including the regulations governing how you document, such as Meaningful Use, ICD-10, and others
- Your support staff and your relationships and leadership abilities in organizing your team
- Your compensation formula
- Your relationships with physician colleagues and administrative leadership
- The industry consolidation and competition in your local area. It is not uncommon to find yourself in a group that is selling to a larger group, sometimes for the second or third time in as many years.
- Your call rotation and confidence in your partner's abilities to adequately care for your patients
- The uncertainty and threat of overwhelming patient volumes brought into play by the Affordable Care Act (Obamacare) and the shift from volume to value in the US

And on and on and on it goes. Add any remaining stresses you are feeling in your current job to the end of this large list.

These additional job-associated stresses can make shutting the exam room door—and having your seven-and-a-half minutes with the patient—an island of sanity in what feels like a crazy career choice.

These stresses hit below the belt as well. The only way to deal with them effectively is to use skill sets you were never taught.

Your Missing Skill Sets

Residency trains you to be a competent clinician. Within your specialty, you are experienced in taking a history, diagnosing and ordering treatment, and follow-up for a core matrix of illnesses. Now that you are a working physician, your job responsibilities could really use several additional skill sets. There was no room in residency to teach you these, and they would really come in handy now. Here is a partial list:

- Leadership
- Project management

- Business development
- Business finance
- Team communication

(To name a few.)

When you add these stresses to the stress of just seeing patients, your workday can quickly force you into survival mode. You become laser-focused on simply getting to your last patient with the minimum of hassle. Unfortunately, that is often when your staff punches out and goes home, leaving you behind to finish up the charting—sometimes in the office, and too often at home after dinner as well.

Job-related stresses differ by practice model.

The stresses you experience from your job are often determined by the business model of your practice. Job-related stress is universal; the "flavor" of the stress is different depending on whether your practice model is:

- Solo
  - › Insured practice
  - › Direct pay or concierge practice
- Physician-owned small group (no practice administrator)
- Physician-owned larger group (with an administrator or CEO)
  - › Single specialty
  - › Multi-specialty
- Large employer
  - › Independent
  - › Hospital-based
  - › Profit
  - › Not-for-profit

The smaller your practice, the more your stress will come from hiring, training, managing, and firing people and marketing your services—especially if you are direct pay or concierge.

The larger your practice—especially if you are employed by a large healthcare organization—the more your stress comes from navigating a bureaucracy and the silos of administration vs. clinicians that inevitably form.

Beware of Magical Thinking

You may be tempted to think changing your practice model will eliminate all your stress. You hear this when a physician says something like, "If I was just solo …" or "If I just sell my practice to MegaHealthCorp and become an employee, everything will be so much easier." This is a form of magical thinking. I encourage you to let it go unless you are completely aware of the complete palette of stresses in the new position and are equipped and experienced in successfully dealing with them.

If you do change jobs and practice models, the change rarely brings the stress relief you seek. You simply trade one flavor of stress for another. Often, I meet physicians at the point where they have done exactly this: jump from the frying pan into the fire.

Burnout Cause #3: Having a Life

For most physicians, your larger life is the place where you recharge. You rest and recuperate and make deposits in your energy accounts when you are off the job.

There is a huge assumption here though. We all assume you know *how* to recharge when you are not at work. We both know it is not a skill you were ever actually taught. Sure, you would come home from a long shift as a resident, grab whatever you could to eat, and crash until the next day. But that is not true recharge or authentic life balance.

The 800-Pound Gorilla

Left to its own devices, your career is very much like living with an 800-pound silverback gorilla.

The gorilla patrols your house, taking what it wants and leaving you with only scraps of time and energy. Your career can do exactly the same thing with your life. It can completely dominate your time away from your practice and all your major relationships. It can feel like you only get the cold leftovers to yourself. If it feels that way to you, I wonder how it feels to your spouse or significant other?

The skills to create and maintain life balance are ones you have to learn for yourself by trial and error, all while simultaneously balancing the stresses of the practice of medicine and your specific job.

Life gets much more complicated in our 30s and beyond as well.

Occasionally, residents will marry and start a family before they graduate. However, most of us begin that phase in our lives after taking our first job position. This is usually a huge time and energy demand we never needed to cope with until now.

More examples of the additional stress having a life adds to the mix:

- Your relationship with your spouse or significant other
- Children and raising and caring for a family
- Your own physical health and fitness
- Finances (saving money, paying off debt, investments, buying in as a partner in your group, etc.)
- Your wider family responsibilities, including caring for aging parents, etc.
- Hobbies, friendships, and interests outside of medicine

Most of us are able to grow a life and find some balance by trial and error. We learn to get some exercise and sleep and deal with the additional time commitments of our life outside of medicine. Our skill in this balancing act varies from week-to-week, and everyone is on their own to figure it out.

What if things don't go well?

If anything happening outside of work begins to block your ability to recharge your energy accounts, you are in trouble. These blocks to recharge at home can become burnout at work.

If you are a physician leader, it is important to understand this. High stress levels at home can prevent recharge. This will show up as burnout on the job, even when the problem is not on the job site at all.

If you are a leader checking in with a colleague who seems to be struggling, make sure you ask how things are going at home. Any number of situations at home can present exactly like classic burnout in the workplace.

You won't find the actual cause unless you ask. Here is a partial list of possibilities:

- Conflict in the physician's primary relationship, including separation and divorce
- Birth of a child
- Problems with children—from special needs to behavior issues and more
- Financial hardships
- Personal health issues
- Wider family issues such as the failing health of a parent

Simply asking, "How are things at home?" can expose these burnout causes if they are present.

If you have these additional stressors in your life, it is vitally important to continue to take good care of yourself, despite the extra stress and responsibility at home. The first law of burnout applies here, too. When it comes to successfully navigating these life stresses, "You can't give what you ain't got." In some cases, you will need to cut back on work responsibilities to have the time and energy to deal with these issues in your life outside of medicine.

Burnout Cause #4: The Conditioning of Our Medical Education

When I first started coaching burned-out doctors, I often ran into mysterious brick walls. I would point out something obvious they were doing to make themselves miserable, and it appeared they were incapable of seeing what I was seeing. It was talking to a fish about water again.

It became clear over time that physicians have a network of Swiss cheese holes in their awareness. I saw it clearly from the outside, only because I had been out of the day-to-day of clinical practice for several years.

The general public sees these unique features of physician awareness as well. Often, they think this is just how doctors are. You can hear it in their language: *doctors are such workaholics* or other similar pronouncements.

From my perspective, it is clear that doctors are not born this way. I get to know my coaching clients as people very quickly. It is clear to me there is no such thing as a typical doctor personality. The people underneath the MD are always unique and as varied as any segment of the normal population.

Yet, as doctors, we are actually conditioned to think and act in a very similar fashion from physician to physician.

Medical Education is a Conditioning Process

We are taught to play the role of doctor in a very specific and standardized way. It was only when I recognized I was witnessing true conditioning—brainwashing, if you will—that I was able to change my coaching. Understanding that subconscious conditioning was driving their behavior—ambushing them from a blind spot in their awareness—made all the difference.

Five Flavors of Physician Conditioning

Here are the five major "flavors" of conditioning I see in physicians. There are many more minor aspects of conditioning physicians exhibit, but these are the big five that most commonly get in the way of our happiness.

1. Workaholic
2. Superhero
3. Emotion-free
4. Lone Ranger
5. Perfectionist

Before they became subconscious conditioning, we learned each of these as distinct and very useful skill sets. Let's face it—there were hundreds of times in your medical education the skills of a workaholic or perfectionist or a person who is capable of being emotion-free came in handy. In fact, you could not have become a physician without them.

In an ideal world, you would have been taught to use them the way a carpenter uses the tools on his belt. You pull out a hammer when it is the best tool for the job at hand. You use it to drive in that nail, and then you slide it back into the loop on your tool belt where it belongs. When you are done with your power tool, you turn it off and put it away.

When you are done with work, you take your tool belt off and put it away until your next day on the job.

Those are healthy boundaries.

Early in our training, we hone and practice these skill sets constantly. We become experts in their use, even as pre-meds. We need them just to survive the training process of medical school and then residency.

Here is one of the differences between a doctor and a carpenter: no one ever showed you how to turn your tools off and put them away. We have no tool belt we can simply unclip and hang on a hook when we get home.

Very early in our education, we actually become our tools.

We become workaholic, superhero, emotion-free, Lone Ranger perfectionists. Without knowing how to turn them off and put them away, we start to live our whole lives this way. People outside of medicine look at doctors and think, *That's just the way doctors are.* What they are really seeing is this deep, comprehensive, and subconscious conditioning. This is one of the prices we pay to survive the education process. It sets us up for burnout down the road.

Recognizing Your Programming

- You can recognize your workaholic programming when your only solution to any problem is to work harder, and you get angry at people who don't work as hard as you.
- You can recognize the superhero when you feel you should save everyone or get very upset when you can't.
- Your emotion-free programming is in play when you notice you have feelings about a specific patient—and immediately feel guilty or inadequate for not being emotion-free and detached.
- You can recognize the Lone Ranger when you are stuck in the maze of doing everything yourself, despite having a team around you.
- You can recognize the perfectionist when you agonize over details that are not clinically relevant or chastise patients and your staff for minor imperfections.

If you happen to be an overstressed and burned out physician, this programming actively gets in your way when you are trying to turn the downward spiral around. One of the keys to your recovery is recognizing the difference between your voice and the voices of these programmed pieces of your doctor persona.

But wait. There's more.

The Physician's Two Prime Directives

In addition to the five main "flavors" of programming listed above, we are deeply conditioned to operate by two prime directives.

1. "The patient comes first."

This mantra sets up a pecking order. Patient first...me somewhere down the line. This is in direct conflict with the first law of burnout: *you can't give what you ain't got.*

Your ability to care for a patient is completely dependent upon maintaining a positive balance in your energy accounts. The patient simply cannot always come first. You must have time where you put yourself first in order to recharge. This makes the same sense as third grade addition and this basic truth seems to be hidden in most healthcare workplaces.

This prime directive is a direct block to recharging.

If you operate by the principle of *the patient comes first* at all times, this mindset is a major cause of your stress and burnout. It is the source of your guilty feelings when you actually block out time for yourself and do something "selfish" like read a book or take a nap.

The thought that this activity is selfish comes from your workaholic programming. You see that, yes?

If you look at other professions that put their "client" first, you will have a who's who of the highest burnout industries. A partial list includes hotel, restaurant, and other hospitality categories, healthcare, law enforcement, and active-duty military.

The patient comes first is a recipe for burnout if there is no off switch or protected space from its command.

2. "Never show weakness."

If you have any doubts this is true for physicians, consider this scenario:

Remember back when you were a resident. If your chief looked at you and said, "Hey, how are you doing? You look beat. Is everything okay?" what would you have said in return? Be honest.

We both know the answer to that question. It would go something like this:

"What? I'm fine. Right as rain. Couldn't be better. What's up? You have another admission? I'll take it. Gimme two, they're small." Or something along those lines.

Our training is a gladiator-style survival process. The last one standing is the chief. If you show signs that you "can't take it," you are shuffled off to the side and avoided like a leper.

This conditioning never goes away. It actively blocks our ability to recognize when we are not okay. It completely blocks our ability to ask for help, no matter how far into the downward spiral of burnout you may be. I personally believe it is part of the reason doctors' suicide rates are higher than the general population.

No one tried to do this to you.

It is important to note that despite the power and the comprehensive nature of the conditioning of our training, no one ever actually conspired to condition you. The faculty in your training program did not plot to instill these blind spots in the doctor's lounge while you were out on the wards. There is no one to blame here.

The power of this conditioning is immense.

The key to the depth of our brainwashing is the intensity and length of the education process we use to produce a board certified physician.

Do you know anything about basic training in the military? It lasts six to twelve weeks, depending on the branch of service. We all know basic training is a conditioning process, right? By the time that brief but intense process is through, an eighteen-year-old recruit will walk into a live fire exercise when asked to do so. The only reason they follow that insane request is because their conditioning now sees that as an "order" they must follow.

Minus the deadly weapons, do you think your medical education was any less intense than military training? Add up the years between your first day of medical school and the day you became board certified. How long was that for you? In the US, it is a minimum of seven years, and I have seen surgeons with up to seventeen years of training.

Do you think it is possible you were conditioned just a tiny little bit in that time?

Recognize and De-Program

Let's restore some balance to the force here. Try this exercise to reveal some of the programming you absorbed since the day you started medical school. This will help you begin letting go of the pieces of the programming that are not healthy.

I encourage you to read, contemplate, and journal on the following paragraphs.

- It is okay—in fact, it is absolutely necessary—to take care of my personal needs for sleep, nutrition, exercise, and time with the people I love. This is not being selfish. I don't need to feel guilty. I must recharge for one simple reason: *you can't give what you ain't got.*

- It is okay—normal, in fact—to have times when I am down, struggling, trashed, and need a break. At those times, it is okay to tell someone and ask for help and support. I am not being weak, a pussy, a wimp, or in a situation of not being able to take it.

- It is okay to delegate tasks to my team. I don't have to—and simply can't—do it all myself.

- There are many places in life where good enough is good enough. I don't always have to be perfect. Instead of always being perfect, I can ask myself, *Is perfection necessary here*? If not, I can take a breath and let it go.

- The patient cannot always come first. That is insane. It is a recipe for burnout. I can learn how to create a boundary between work and home and create time when family and I come first.
- I don't have to have all the answers. I can lead by asking questions and tap the power of my patients, their families, and my larger team.
- It is impossible to avoid feeling emotions when I am taking care of my patients. To be emotion-free is incompatible with caring. I know will have emotions, and I know it is okay to feel them. I can learn how to feel and not be drained or weakened by my feelings.

BURNOUT BASICS SUMMARY

1. The Practice: The stress of the clinical practice of medicine.
2. The Job: The stresses of your specific job position that are independent of the stress of seeing patients.
3. Having a Life: The stress of maintaining your physical health, building and maintaining life balance, and the ability to recharge your energy accounts when you are not at work.
4. The Programming of Our Medical Education:
    - Workaholic—Superhero—Emotion-Free—Lone Ranger—Perfectionist
    - "The patient comes first"
    - "Never show weakness"

Your new awareness can make a big difference.

Simply being aware of this programming will help you notice when it pops into your awareness and the habits it has created. I hope you can also see how your medical education did not teach you about three of these four causes of burnout. Unfortunately, most doctors don't learn about burnout until after they are suffering from it. Now, you are fully informed and will be able to see the causes of burnout in real time as you notice them in the days, weeks, and years ahead.

Share This Knowledge

I strongly encourage you to share this chapter with your spouse or significant other. Remember, much of this lies hidden in your blind spots. Your spouse or significant other is your early warning system for burnout behavior when you are in survival mode and revert to pure programming.

WHAT DOES THE EXPERIENCE OF BURNOUT FEEL LIKE?

"Burnout …an erosion of the soul caused by a deterioration of one's values, dignity, spirit and will."
—Christina Maslach

WHEN WE TALK about the symptoms of burnout, we are in a third-person perspective. It is like talking about the symptoms of a heart attack when you are observing another person having one. This is the normal perspective of the practicing physician. You are helping other people understand and treat their symptoms. Being a doctor is not about you and your symptoms.

Then, there's burnout.

You must be able to recognize the primary experience for yourself and understand what to do about it. Now, I do not recommend you try to diagnose and treat your own chest pain; however, I do recommend you be on the lookout for burnout at all times. It is one of the few times you must self-diagnose or listen carefully to your spouse or significant other. Recognizing your own burnout as it is happening is another missing skill set from our medical education—especially for men—and one of the primary reasons I wrote this book.

Let's talk about what it feels like to experience burnout from a first-person perspective—not a scholarly discussion of symptoms, but what you are thinking and feeling when you look in the mirror in the morning, your energy accounts tapped dry, dreading another day in the office.

Survival mode

When your energy accounts drop below zero, your subconscious silently switches into survival mode. You can tell this by noticing the following thought pattern: *I just want to get through the day.*

You know you are in survival mode when you look at today's schedule and can think of only one thing: *How can I make it to the end of these patients as quickly as possible and get out of here?*

In survival mode, you will tend to be upset with anything or anyone who presents a complication, hassle, or interruption to getting the work done. These frustrations will sneak out your mouth in the form of cynicism or sarcasm and other verbal signs of compassion fatigue.

Your staff, patients, and family may see it as a stiffening of your posture when someone tells you, "Mavis Thornapple just called, and she is coming in with a rash," or something similar. Inside, you may or may not recognize frustration, extreme fatigue, anger (to the point of fury), hopelessness, and a whole host of negative emotions.

Your physiology and subconscious thought processes are focused on survival. They see your work as the source of an energy drain that is threatening the integrity of you as an organism. They are shutting down your higher functions so you can maintain a minimal additional energy drain and still function as a clinician.

When you are at home, you may find it very difficult to shut off your thoughts about your practice. This is especially true if you are not an EMR power user and are doing work at home in the off-hours; or, if you have not learned how to disconnect yourself from practice technology like your smart phone.

If thoughts come up about how you are feeling, you may notice a voice saying things like:

> *I'm not sure how much longer I can go on like this.*
> *I don't understand what is happening here. I keep working harder and harder, but it's like I can't ever catch up.*
> *This is crazy. This is not what I thought my career would be like.*
> *Am I crazy? Is something wrong with me?*
> *If this keeps going, I'm afraid I am going to make a mistake and someone will get hurt.*

Your significant other and other family members may notice your exhaustion and dissatisfaction and comment on it. They may have been commenting on your stress for years now. You will most likely attempt to soldier on or figure it out for yourself. You were trained to respond in this way. This is workaholic, superhero, Lone Ranger, "never show weakness" programming at its finest.

In some cases, your colleagues and/or the administrators of your group may talk to you about your energy and attitude. This occurs most often when your burnout leads to outbursts of what they see as disruptive behavior. This is far more common if you are a man. The complaints about your words or actions can come from staff members, colleagues, or patients. Typically, you feel bad about the incidents they call you out on while justifying what you did or said as a reasonable response given the situation.

Taking time off cannot reverse burnout

Here is a lesson I learned the hard way and a common mistake many physicians make: you may take a break, thinking you just need to "recharge your batteries." Now, you know better. When you understand the energy account mechanism of burnout, you know taking a break only provides temporary relief.

Whether you take a long weekend, an extended vacation, a full-on sabbatical, or go to a conference or retreat in an effort to recharge those batteries, you will find your energy is only temporarily improved. You will be back in the exhaustion of survival mode very soon upon your return. It cannot be any other way. To remain in a positive balance in your energy accounts, you must change the actions that drained you in the first place. Lower your stress levels, increase your ability to recharge, or both.

Without significant changes in your actions, your energy accounts may bounce back above zero (assuming you know how to recharge in the time you take off), but when you return to work, what does your energy do? Yes, it will eventually fall back below zero again.

The natural history of burnout

There are several directions burnout can take once it sets in:

- You can recognize it, change your actions/habits/routines, and your relationship with your career to recover.
- It can become a chronic condition, often accompanied by disruptive behavior.
- You can suffer a complication such as alcohol or other substance abuse, divorce, depression, or suicide.
- You can quit making a living as a physician by either changing careers or retiring.

The rest of this book will focus on option one above: recognize and recover. Before I show you several ways to get your energy accounts into a positive balance, though, I encourage you to aim higher than just treating or preventing burnout.

Let me show you how to put burnout to its highest and best use.

WHAT IS BURNOUT'S HIGHEST AND BEST USE?

"It's better to burnout
than to fade away."
—Neil Young

"At every single moment of one's life,
one is what one is going to be
no less than what one has been."
—Oscar Wilde

FROM WITHIN THE misery of physician burnout, it is difficult to see the possibility of a purpose to this suffering. Let me reassure you, though, that burnout actually has a highest and best use. When you do a good job of recovering from burnout, you will look back on this as the point when everything turned for the better. Rather than fight burnout or fall victim to it, you can use it to stop the downward spiral, creating a new and better reality for yourself and your family in the process.

Here's how I know this: I have worked with hundreds of burned-out doctors and physician leaders at this point, and a clear and universal pattern has emerged. Let me show it to you.

Try this snippet of anthropologic research

Think of a physician you respect and look up to, someone you feel has his or her act together in work and private life. Ask if you can have a cup of coffee and a conversation. When you are together, I encourage you to make this request:

"Please, tell me your burnout story."

Most likely, the reply will be something along the lines of, "Which one?"

I encourage you to listen to the story you are told. It will be of a turning point where this person finally stepped away from a situation that was not working. The story often ends with something like, " …and thank God that happened, or I would still be back in that grind and none of this would be possible."

Burnout marks the normal passages of life

Here is my experience after talking with hundreds of physicians in all specialties: The lifetime incidence of physician burnout is right around 100 percent.

It seems that people don't often get their acts together without burnout. Burnout marks the place where you have followed someone else's path long enough that your body is telling you change is necessary in ways you can no longer ignore. You finally pull your head up and realize beyond any doubt that this is not your path.

If you continue on this route, you will violate your own values, deny the people you love, and most likely slide into a "life of quiet desperation." Burnout gets you to finally say, "I can't do this anymore. There has to be another way."

Unless you turn the downward spiral around before this crisis point, physician burnout will eventually push you to near breaking. I hope and pray that when you reach that point, you bend and spring back rather than snap like some of the unfortunate among our brothers and sisters. Alcohol, drugs, depression, other mental illnesses, and suicide are all complications I hope you avoid. The good news is that it is only a tiny minority of physicians will face those trials.

The rest of us are left with a scene Robert Frost described best. You can see that there is more than one option available. It is clear you are free to choose between the two. Either choice has its own set of unique consequences.

> *"Two roads diverged in a wood that day and I,*
> *I took the one less traveled by*
> *And that has made all the difference."*
> —Robert Frost

At this point, when you have no energy left to keep putting out the fires of other people's demands and priorities, something important happens. You realize with undeniable clarity that you have other choices available, and the path you have been on all this time is simply one choice among many.

Then, reality hits you like a brick wall.

1. You can keep fighting all the things that you don't want. You can keep trying to fix the problems by working harder.
Or,
2. You can decide what you really want in your practice, your life, and your relationships with the people you love. You can get crystal clear on that instead …and go get it.

No matter how far you have gone on a wrong road, turn back.
—Turkish proverb

The train on someone else's tracks

It is as if you became a little train engine on your first day of medical school and climbed onto a set of tracks someone else had laid down. The tracks led in a straight line to your medical degree. The only way off was to derail yourself. We all know someone who fell off the tracks along the way, but that was not you.

In residency, you moved to a new set of tracks that led you to board certification. There was no wiggle room. If you played the game by the residency rules, you ended up with your boards and finished your medical education.

In your job, you switched to another set of tracks. These are the rails of "the way we do things around here." These are still not your tracks. You did not lay them. However, just like a good resident or med student, you chugged down the tracks until it became clear they were headed in a direction that didn't give you the fulfillment and life balance you dreamed of in your training. It was supposed to be different once you had your boards …right? Here's what you missed.

You didn't realize that you don't have to run on anyone else's tracks anymore. You have the skills and ability to take your practice in a number of directions now. You can design and implement your practice and your larger life from now on. Honest.

Burnout is when you figure out how to lay your own tracks, or, better yet, realize you are a four-wheel-drive vehicle—not a train confined to its tracks. You can navigate any terrain you choose. The way you have been doing things up until now is only one of the options available.

Physician burnout is hard-wired into doctors

Much of the struggle and ultimate crisis of physician burnout is rooted in human neuroanatomy and the conditioning of our medical education.

We are creatures of habit. Most of our habits as practicing physicians were instilled deep in our subconscious by the medical education process. And we cannot deny that our human wiring and gender play a role.

- We are wired deep in the reticular activating system to be on the lookout for and avoid pain and danger. The two basic animal instincts are to move toward pleasure and away from pain. The avoidance of pain is a much stronger impulse. It is a foundational feature of our human behavior and neuroanatomy.

- Our medical education teaches us to see danger everywhere. Everyone is sick until proven otherwise. Each patient encounter offers the opportunity for a missed diagnosis and disaster. The basic act of a differential diagnosis raises catastrophizing and paranoia to an art form.
- We are conditioned in residency to be workaholic, superhero, emotion-free, Lone Ranger perfectionists. No one shows us the off switch.
- Since the first day of medical school, we have been 100 percent focused on doing what other people want us to do. Despite exhaustion, sleep deprivation, burnout, come hell or high water, we get the job done, because the patient comes first, dammit.

With this as a backdrop, we face all challenges/problems/issues/concerns in our lives in the same way. We work harder in an attempt to bulldoze the problem with sheer will and massive effort.

Good luck with that. It is an old habit pattern. It won't work with everything. It won't give you any quality of life. Your significant other won't love you more for this tendency of yours.

Then physician burnout wears you down to a nub

Your ability to continue on these tracks and this path falls away.

Here is where meaningful change can start. It can come in the form of a full-blown crisis or by conscious choice triggered by the realization that you simply cannot go on like this. I sincerely hope you fall into the latter category when your time comes.

Here is a way to begin that has been proven in my own life and with hundreds of our coaching clients, in the real world of clinical medicine.

Time to Do the "Big 180"

In order to see the way through, you must step out of your programming and make a 180-degree shift in your awareness.

Move from avoiding the things you don't want …

…to figuring out what you really want …

…and going to get it.

No problem can be solved
from the same level of consciousness that created it.
—Albert Einstein

I often get asked, "If I can just avoid all the things I don't want, I will get what I want …right?" What do you think the answer is?

Here is the reality

To get what you want, the steps you need to take will look something like this:

1. Take the time to decide what you want in your life and career.
2. Start taking baby steps in that direction, beginning to free up your purpose.
3. Wake up the dreams you tucked away when you entered medical school.
4. Get off the tracks others have laid for you to follow.
5. Put physician burnout to its highest and best use.

Burnout is here to nudge you onto your own path. You really can set your own tracks from now on. You can use your discomfort to fuel your change.

The remainder of this book is devoted to giving you new levels of awareness and teaching new tools. You will learn how to step off these rails of others' expectations. Let me show you how to recognize your own path and navigate its twists and turns toward your Ideal Practice with intention and on purpose.

Perhaps you will become like that wise and respected mentor I asked you to think about at the beginning of this chapter. Perhaps you will share your burnout story with others down the road.

When you are ready to get started, let's take out the trash.

Burnout's highest and best use ACTION STEPS

- What choices do you see available to you now?
- What are the consequences of each path you might take going forward?
- What do you really want at this point in your life and your career?
- Is now the time to take action and go get it?
- If so, what is the first step on the path ahead?
- Journal on your answers to these questions.

CHAPTER 2

TAKE OUT THE HEAD TRASH

Five Changes in Awareness that Enable the Burnout Prevention
Tools to Work

"It ain't what you don't know that gets you into trouble.
It's what you know for sure that just ain't so."
—Mark Twain

"We don't see things as they are, we see them as we are."
—Anaïs Nin

"He that will not apply new remedies must expect new evils."
—Francis Bacon

Head trash is the trash in your head. It is the crooked and inaccurate thought processes, the smoke and mirrors of your conditioning that all get in your way without you knowing it. I have already shown you five flavors of programming and two prime directives that set every doctor up to be at extremely high risk for burnout. That is one category of head trash. Let me show you five additional, doctor-specific behavior patterns and world views that will also get in your way, so we can take them out to the Dumpster all at once.

Do not skip this chapter.

You must take out the trash before you have any chance of living on purpose. Empty the trash, and then we can instill the new tools that follow into the bright, shiny space you will create. Just like cleaning the kitchen before you prepare a new dish for the first time, taking out the head trash first provides you with a fresh start and a foundation for a new and upward spiral.

HEAD TRASH #1: DEAL WITH YOUR INNER CRITIC

As you learn about burnout and contemplate new actions, you will probably notice a voice in your head now and then we can call your "inner critic." It is a part of your personality that judges you and can get in the way of taking new action steps. Its dominant emotion is usually guilt or shame.

Here are some examples of what your inner critic might whisper in your ear:

> *Jeez, why didn't you know this sooner? You are such an idiot.*
> *You can't take time for yourself; that's selfish.*
> *Like that is ever going to happen.*
> *This is too difficult/simple/stupid/woo woo.*
> *I am too busy for any of this.*

Whatever your inner critic says, the key is to not let that little voice stop you from making the changes you are seeking. Try this first: When you hear the little voice trying to take you out, say to yourself, *Thank you for sharing*, and keep moving forward.

One of two things will happen:

1. **The inner critic will let you pass.** It will come up again at some point, and your *thank you for sharing* will continue to be enough that it will step aside and allow you to proceed.

If you find your inner critic is either absent or it does not stop you from moving forward, things are simpler. Carry on, full speed ahead. You can move on to the next section, Head Trash #2.

If option (2) below is happening to you, please take a moment to read the next few paragraphs carefully.

2. **The inner critic will hijack you.** Let's look at this in some detail on the off chance this is happening to you right now.

What do I mean by "hijack?"

You will be stopped by a powerful negative emotion and not allowed to proceed. In your body, it feels the way a kitten must feel when you grab it by the skin of the back of its neck and lift it off the floor.

- If you try *thank you for sharing* several times with your inner critic's objections, and it will not stand aside and let you proceed;

Or,

- If you are hijacked as above when trying to make changes, especially if this sense of panic seems familiar or you are unable to control your emotions;

You have legitimate reasons for a visit to a therapist or coach with experience in what is known as "parts work." This powerful inner critic is a "part" of your personality. "Parts work" is the name for a number of techniques that help you bring all the parts of your personality onto the same page and get them all pulling in the same direction.

In about 20 percent of my coaching clients, there is an inner critic that will not allow things to proceed until we upgrade their relationship with the critic. In most cases, something traumatic happened during their medical education or their practice years that resonates with a trauma from childhood. This kind of head trash is important to recognize right away. It is often difficult to take it out without some professional help.

If you try to Lone Ranger here, it is not uncommon to get stopped in your tracks or confused enough to give up on your attempts to change things for the better. I encourage you to ask for help and allow yourself to be supported in this situation, especially if you happen to be a man.

Please realize that in these situations, your inner critic is trying to protect you. It is a blunt and effective instrument to stop you in your tracks. It uses old tactics and phrases that probably sound familiar. It is afraid of changing because it doesn't understand that the changes you are trying to make will be good for both of you.

You and your coach or therapist can work on bringing your relationship with this inner critic up to adult standards. When this is done well, this same voice will transform into your biggest ally and a key inner source of advice and wisdom.

As a coach, I have done this work in my own life. Learning to work with my own inner critic and other parts of my personality was the key to my recovery from burnout. I am skilled and experienced in several parts work methods and can offer some suggestions for how you might proceed if your inner critic is blocking your progress.

Feel free to contact me through this link for a free Discovery Session consult: ***www.thehappymd.com/contact***.

HEAD TRASH #2: REALIZE BURNOUT IS NOT A PROBLEM

BURNOUT IS A challenge to be sure. It is not a problem, though. Here's what I mean:

PROBLEMS HAVE SOLUTIONS.

When you apply the solution to a problem, what happens? The problem disappears, right?

Problem + Solution = No Problem

Example:

Here is the purest example of a problem I can think of for a practicing physician: an abscess.

What is the treatment for an abscess, especially if it is one of those beauties that is just starting to point? You got it …drainage. In the language of the surgeon, "a chance to cut is a chance to cure."

There is no finer example of a one-step solution than the application of a surgical blade to the burrowing head of a ripening abscess.

So an abscess is a problem.

Abscess + Drainage = No Abscess

You wash your hands, clean your instruments, smile, and thank the gods of medicine that you got a simple problem like this in your work day.

What about burnout? Is there the equivalent of a scalpel you can use to I&D burnout and make it go away? The answer is an obvious "no." There is no one-step, permanent solution here.

The Important Distinction

- The reason you can't find a solution for burnout is *not* because burnout is impossible to prevent.
- The reason there is no solution is this—burnout is not a problem.

• **Burnout is a Dilemma.**

di·lem·ma noun \də-'le-mə *A situation in which a difficult choice has to be made between two alternatives—especially when both alternatives are either undesirable or mutually incompatible.*

In common language, we speak of being on the "horns of a dilemma."

The Balancing Act

Dealing successfully with a dilemma is a constant process of finding balance between the horns. In this instance, burnout is actually one of the horns. There are two alternatives in this particular dilemma.

DILEMMA: PRODUCTIVITY VS. BURNOUT

If you push your productivity too hard, you burn out and productivity falls. What you and your employer are seeking is a healthy balance of solid productivity at work without driving your energy account balances below zero and causing burnout. This is true whether you are employed by a large organization or are a solo practitioner.

How do you "solve" a dilemma?

The short answer here is you don't.
• You *solve* problems.
• You *manage* dilemmas.

Your ability to distinguish between problems and dilemmas is a key new skill that will allow you to treat and prevent burnout. This problem vs. dilemma distinction is one you must learn to see clearly in order to build a fulfilling, balanced life.

Power Tip:
**Any time you find yourself struggling to "solve a problem,"
question your assumptions.**

**Ask, "Is this a problem or a dilemma?" and proceed accordingly.
Learning to recognize and manage dilemmas makes your life easier.**

Four steps to manage a dilemma

Once you recognize you are facing a dilemma and not a problem—as in the case at hand, dealing with burnout—use these four steps to manage it effectively.

1. **DEFINE** the two horns and the optimum balance point.
2. Design a **STRATEGY** to create the balance you seek.
3. Build a **SYSTEM** to monitor the effectiveness of your strategy.
4. **TWEAK** your strategy and your system as often as needed.

THREE PROBLEM-SOLVING TRAPS FOR DOCTORS

We are problem solvers by our nature, our training, and our conditioning. We are always looking for a solution to our patients' symptoms. We have a finely-honed sense of urgency as well. Because of the length of the typical patient encounter, we do everything we can to tease out the unifying diagnosis and build an effective treatment plan in fifteen minutes or less.

We tend to see everything as a problem and we derive our sense of worth and confidence from our ability to solve the problems around us.

Then, there's burnout. We make the mistake of thinking burnout is a problem, too. We try to solve it over and over again and are unsuccessful. This is where a whole new layer of head trash tumbles in.

Instead of going back to the drawing board and questioning our assumptions, we fall into three main patterns of dysfunctional behavior. Rather than recognize burnout as a dilemma and work on a strategy, a large percentage of physicians will do one of these three things instead.

1. Give Up

If you can't find a solution, it must be impossible. You look all around and see many of your colleagues struggling in a similar fashion. Your programming has you work harder and try to figure this out all by yourself, despite your exhaustion. Eventually, many physicians simply give up on the option of having the life they want. Burnout is often a chronic condition.

2. Play the Victim

Much more commonly, physicians slide into playing the role of the victim. I am not saying you are being victimized here. There is no perpetrator. No one is sitting in a smoke-filled room plotting to knock your life out of balance and deliberately torture you with EMR, ICD-10, Meaningful Use, or patient satisfaction surveys.

Victim mode is a creeping change in your locus of control. You begin to believe you are not in charge of your life. You feel like you are swinging in the breeze, a helpless victim of the next administration order that comes down the pike.

The following behaviors are three signs you are playing the victim:

1. Blame
2. Justify
3. Complain

Any time you find yourself doing one of these, you are playing the victim. In most cases, you missed a chance along the way to take more charge of your circumstances. Now, you feel stuck. You don't see a solution, so these feel like reasonable things to do. You are giving your power away. This behavior is very common among physicians, as you well know.

Playing the victim is learned helplessness.

Blaming, justifying, and complaining never work. These three behaviors will never get you what you want. You will only alienate the very same people that could help you out of the downward spiral.

Did you know there is a popular conception in healthcare management circles that doctors are just a bunch of whiners? Listen to their stories and you will see that many administrators are bombarded with physicians who do nothing but walk into their office to blame, justify, and complain about everything. They demand something be done about the issue at hand and storm out. And I am not even talking about the so-called "disruptive doctors" here. The constant repetition of victim behaviors is what causes administrators to give up on burnout prevention and deal with physician turnover instead.

Playing the victim is one of the few things that is more common in doctors than the symptoms of burnout themselves. This head trash has got to go if you are going to get more of what you want going forward.

You can un-learn this behavior.

Doing so will make a big difference for a simple reason. When you blame, justify, and complain, you are giving away your power to change things. Instead of figuring out what you want and making it happen, you are venting your discomfort and putting up with this miserable status quo.

Playing the victim means you missed an opportunity to take charge. When you catch yourself in victim mode, you will realize that at some earlier point you had an opportunity to take control of the situation and you missed it.

You might have noticed the opportunity come up, but you did not take it. Or, you might have missed it completely. Either way, recognizing you are playing the victim gives you a second chance to take charge.

- What do you really want to have happen here—instead of the thing you are complaining about?
- What would you have to do to get that different result?
- What is the smallest first step you can take to begin turning this around?
- When are you going to do *that* instead of blame, justify, and complain?

I encourage you to recognize the victim when it pops up. Use it as a sign to get crystal clear on what you want in this situation. Then, take charge of the situation as much as possible.

3. Pray for a Magic Pill

Everyone yearns for the magic pill, for snake oil, for a cure-all. It comes out of doctors' mouths when they say things like, "Just tell me what to do to make EMR go away, and I'll do it."

There is no magic pill, especially when we are talking about burnout. Here is my experience:

- The origin of burnout is always multifactorial.
- A successful strategy for the treatment and prevention of burnout is always multifactorial.
- Creating your ideal practice and an amazing life is always multifactorial.

There is no one thing. There is no magic pill, no matter how much you may wish for it. The magic pill is a universal form of magic thinking. The key is to recognize the dilemma and focus on taking action in the form of a strategy to pull up.

Let It Go

Treating or preventing burnout or building your ideal practice is always a combination of a number of little changes. Clean out your head trash and put together several new actions that get the results you are seeking.

As long as you remain focused on what you want and dedicated to taking action to implement the tools in your life, you will find that every new action produces a new result. The results of your new actions often add up in an exponential fashion. When you begin to live more on purpose and take actions to create your ideal practice, as little as two small changes can make a huge impact.

Get ready to put a number of things in play, one at a time. Then, you can sit back and watch the math of your new results take place.

Know You Have a Strategic Partner Now

Now that you understand burnout is a dilemma, you can recognize this book and the additional resources in the Power Tools Library on the web at ***www.thehappymd.com/powertools*** as the building blocks for your strategy. You build your own personal strategy by picking and choosing the ones that work for you and trying them in your own practice and life. You will quickly learn which combination works best to reach your goals.

Burnout is Not the Only Dilemma You are Facing Right Now

I will point out additional dilemmas as we bump into them going forward. You will recognize them as stubborn places where you are struggling at the moment. Just to get you started, realize that EMR and work-life balance are both dilemmas, too. Go figure.

I will be reminding you to stop trying to solve dilemmas and work on a balance strategy instead, giving you examples of successful strategies as we go along.

Taking out this head trash by calling out dilemmas when you see them is perhaps the most important trip to the Dumpster of them all.

HEAD TRASH #3: DO THE BIG 180

WE TOUCHED ON this in the last chapter, and it is a piece of head trash that cannot be emphasized enough. In order to get what you want, you have to stop the natural and constant focus on avoiding what you don't want.

We are hard-wired at the level of the reticular activating system to be on the look-out for danger and threats. We have a default setting in our neuroanatomy to focus our awareness on our problems. We see the things that are not going right like giant neon lights on a dark night.

The conditioning of our medical education then piles in to form a dense second layer of problem focused awareness.

Example:

If you and I were standing side by side, leaning on the railing of the balcony at Grand Central Station in New York City, looking out over the thousands of people bustling between trains, in the same instant we would both notice the single individual in the crowd who is limping. We would then proceed to get into a heated back and forth discussion over whether his hip or his knee was the source of the problem.

You know this is true. I want you to know something clearly. Only doctors do that kind of thing. We might miss any number of sweet, tender, and touching things going on at the same time. To us, the slight limp seventy-five yards away in the crowd is a flashing red light in our awareness. This ability to spot the pathology others never see is a valuable skill, but only in certain settings. It is no way to live your life when you could focus on all the things that are going right at the same time.

Focusing on What You Want

Building your ideal practice and a balanced life does not come from solving problems. The key is to focus on what you want.

- When you focus on your problems, your attention is occupied by the things you don't want.
- When you focus on your problems, you are looking for things to run away from and avoid.
- Focusing only on the negativity in your life is going to attract more negativity.

- You can fix all your problems and still not get what you want in your life.
- You can toss out this head trash and learn to take a 180-degree turn in your energy and awareness by focusing instead on what you really want and heading in that direction.

Rise Above Neuroanatomy and Programming

I encourage you to rise above the basic reflexes of your reticular activating system and your physician programming and set aside some regular time to focus on what you want.

- I know you took a lot of your dreams and desires and did the spiritual equivalent of stuffing them deep in your back pocket when you entered medical school. We all did.
- I understand no one has ever asked you want you really want, and you probably don't think about it much, given how busy you are.
- Now is a time those dreams and desires can begin to wake up again. You can use them to generate clarity and power as you learn to deal with the dilemmas around you.

Joe Jackson lays out the reality as simply as possible:

> *You can't get what you want till you know what you want.*
> *—Joe Jackson*

Once you know what you really want, you can build an action plan to go straight at it. Your desire for this goal will pull you forward. You will be running toward something positive, instead of running away from something negative. Your attention will be occupied by things you desire, by the life you hope to create. With this as your focus and power source, I promise you will make progress.

HEAD TRASH #4: RELEASE THE SUPERHERO— SPIN PLATES INSTEAD

YOU ARE A physician. You are a person who sees problems and fixes them. Your super-hero sense of urgency is very overdeveloped. After all, under normal circumstances, you only have fifteen minutes or so to figure out the patient, their disease, and the treatment plan.

The biggest temptation when you are reading this book will be to try and do too much at once. This is a recipe for overwhelm for one simple reason. You are probably close enough to overwhelm right now that it wouldn't take much to drive you right over the edge. I would hate this book to be the last straw.

Spin plates instead

Remember the *Ed Sullivan Show*? He is rightly famous for introducing the Beatles, Rolling Stones, and others to US television audiences. But, he also had a number of acts that seem ludicrously primitive by today's standards. One of them was a man named Erich Brenn. Mr. Brenn made a living as a plate spinner. You can search his name on YouTube and find the video of the full performance.

He took plates and bowls and spun them atop long dowels until he had thirteen of them going at once.

One Plate at a Time

The secret to the act was simple. He spun up one plate at a time and didn't move on to the second one until plate number one was going full speed.

When you get to the tools section of this book, make sure you follow his plate spinning lead. Think about your strategy, and know you will be using more than one tool by the time you are done. Then pick a tool—just one—and get it spinning full speed and fully operational in your practice and life before moving on to number two.

Do not overload yourself by taking on multiple action steps at once. It is a recipe for failure and a mind trap of our perfectionist, workaholic, superhero programming.

HEAD TRASH #5: CELEBRATE ALL WINS

OUR PHYSICIAN-FOCUS ON problems will often cause low-level worry and suffering in your life and block your ability to connect with others at work and at home. This tendency is hidden in a physician-specific blind spot at the moment. Doctors often mistake this flavor of head trash for doing a good job and keeping everyone on their toes. It is neither. We took a first pass at this issue in the discussion of "focusing on what you want." This version of our perfectionist program goes much deeper, though.

Not only do we focus on what is not working, we are constantly judging ourselves and all the people around us for missing the mark. If all you are doing is seeing what is going wrong and judging people for it, this habitual thought process will drive your quality of life right into the ditch. There is another way.

You can cultivate the ability to see what is working. You can learn to acknowledge and celebrate and be happy for the things that are going right. A huge body of research from the organizational development and parenting literature shows that this mindset is key to new levels of effectiveness as a leader.[7] It is nothing more than your physician programming keeping you laser-focused on what is going wrong, just like watching the limping man in Grand Central Station.

In reality, there is always something going right at the very same time. You can develop the skill of acknowledging what you and all the people around you have accomplished, rather than focusing only on what remains undone.

When you take on these habit patterns, you put a completely different driver at the wheel of your quality of life.

<u>You don't have to give up being a good doctor to be a happier person.</u>

It is important to note that you don't have to deny your ability to identify and solve problems to accomplish this task. You can be a great diagnostician and the first to point out the unifying diagnosis—and, at the same time, acknowledge what you or the patient or your staff member or your child is doing well.

Here is why it is so important to take out this piece of head trash:

If all you do is focus on what is wrong, you are being too hard on yourself, and you are a pain in the rear to everyone on your team. You are difficult to please and a real task master. The tragedy is you probably don't realize it. It slows you and everyone around you down. It is the essence of the phrase, "nose to the grindstone." You grind your face off with a relentless focus on fixing problems and putting out fires, and it just does not have to be that way. In fact, there is plenty of research evidence that acknowledging what is going right on your team is a key to peak performance.[8]

Let me show you three ways to take out this head trash. Each one is an awareness-shifting tool you can use on yourself and the people around you to keep your energy up and make the journey to your goals a pleasant one from now on.

1. Treat Yourself Like a Dog

Do you have a dog? Have you ever had one? Think of that dog now. If you don't have a dog, think of the cutest dog you can. For me it is always a Corgi puppy.

If you came home and that dog met you at the door, eyes bright and tail wagging, what would you do?

You'd probably say something along the lines of, "Aren't you a good boy?" and give it a scratch behind the ears. You'd be pleased it met you at the door and greeted you in such a fashion. You would show your pleasure in clear and obvious ways—ways we often reserve exclusively for our pets.

Now think of the last time you had a task list at work and you completed one of the tasks. How did you treat yourself? What did you do before you moved on to the next item on the list?

Most physicians will answer, "Nothing—I just moved on to the next thing." Some of us cross the item off with a pen or check a box, but there is no further acknowledgment, no scratch behind the ear.

Take a look at these two situations and you will immediately notice:
- You treat your dog better than you do yourself.
- If you treated your dog the way you treat yourself, your dog would probably go live with your neighbor.

"Treat Yourself Like a Dog" Means "Celebrate All Wins"

Why don't you acknowledge yourself when you complete an item on your task list? Why not do a little fist pump or a couple steps of your happy dance? It is just a habit. There are two main categories of habits, and I don't mean the good and the bad.
1. Habits of doing
2. Habits of not doing

You simply have a habit of *not* celebrating your accomplishments. It is a habit of not doing. That is an exhausting habit, especially since there are dozens of things you could be celebrating every single day, like doing a good job with a patient, completing a chart, helping a member of your team, reading to your children, or the experience of your dog coming to meet you at the door. There are so many positive things to celebrate and acknowledge in your day. You won't see them, though, until you rise above your programming to actually be on the lookout for them.

Just like you and I could look out over Grand Central Station and see the man buying his wife flowers instead of the one who is limping.

I encourage you to develop the habit of noticing and celebrating all wins. Do it for yourself. Do it for your team. Do it for your family.

2. The Gap vs. Progress

In any situation where you are trying to reach a goal, the following graphic applies.

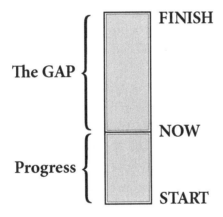

You have a starting point, and the goal is your finish line. At some point, you will be partway there. This sets up two spaces in the diagram.

1. There is a space between where you started and where you are. Let's call that "progress."
2. There is a space between where you are and the finish line. Let's call that "the gap."

Which one of these spaces do you see first?

You are programmed to see the gap more clearly than progress. This is because the gap is the problem. The gap is what is going wrong. We focus on the gap so strongly, it is common to completely ignore or give only passing lip service to progress. We do this with ourselves, our staff, our patients, and our family. The only place we don't have this habit pattern is with our pets—hence, "treat yourself like a dog."

Develop the habit of noticing and celebrating progress first.

You will reach your goals more easily and have more fun along the way. Develop this same habit with your patients, staff, and family, and you will become a better doctor, leader, spouse or significant other, and parent.

I am not saying you should be all *happy happy, joy joy* and ignore the gap. Let's both be realistic here. The gap is the work that has to be done to reach our ultimate goal. Don't ignore or minimize it. Keep the patient and the team organized around closing the gap and reaching your goal. What I am saying is:

- Notice and celebrate progress *first*.
- Congratulate anyone on any progress *first*.
- Reward yourself and others on your accomplishments *first*.

Then, turn to the gap and the issue of how to close it.

Work on the gap; don't beat yourself and everyone up with it.

A Patient Care Example:

Imagine you have a fifty-seven-year-old female patient—Mavis—you have been working up for hypertension. You have worked together to diligently track her blood pressures over the last month, and she is legitimately hypertensive. Your workup for secondary causes is negative. You have decided to start her on medication she must take BID. Two weeks ago, you wrote the prescription and taught her about the medication. She is here in a follow-up visit. Her blood pressure is unchanged on the medication.

> *You: How is the medication going, Mavis?*
>
> *Mavis: I am doing pretty good with the morning dose, Doc, but I'll be darned if I can remember the evening one.*

What would you say next?

My strongest suggestion is you look for something going right in this situation and find a way to treat her like a dog.

You can see the gap, right? You can see what is not going right. You may be getting ready to jump all over that first. I call that *beating her up with the gap*, because that is what it feels like to the patient. That is the way most physicians would handle this. Your frustration leads you to chastise Mavis for the dose she is missing.

If you treat her like a dog first and look for ways to build on what is working, two things will happen. Mavis will enjoy and engage with you and her treatment plan more effectively, and you will have a much more positive and less stressful experience of this patient encounter.

It could go something like this:

> *You: Well Mavis, great job on getting that morning pill into your routine. Well done. What is your secret to remembering that one?*

[Let her respond.]

> *You: Your blood pressures are telling me that we have to work on making your evening pill something you take every day, too. With the success you have had with the morning pill, how would you like to change up your evening routine to make sure you take the evening one, too?*

3. The Satisfaction Mind Flip

- Think about your practice and the way things have been going over the last month or so.
- Rate your level of satisfaction with your practice on a scale of 0–10 (*0 = it couldn't get any worse* and *10 = it couldn't get any better*).
- What is your level of satisfaction?
- How does that number feel?

Notice how your awareness is focused on the problems that keep this score from being a 10. This is a perfect example of how you see the gap first.

When you see your score, what you almost certainly see first is the gap between your score and a 10. If I ask you to list the reasons your satisfaction is not a 10, they come rolling off your tongue in a free-flowing and detailed problem list.

Let's Flip Your Mind Here

Here is the question that triggers the Satisfaction Mind Flip:

Why is your satisfaction score NOT A ZERO?

Grab a sheet of paper and write down all the reasons you didn't give your practice a zero. You know what this list is, yes? It is all the things that are going right in your practice. These are the things you can build on to give you higher levels of satisfaction more quickly than you can imagine.

The quickest way to lower your stress and find more fulfillment in your practice and balance in your life is to figure out what is going right and do more of that.

<u>The Full Triad</u>

1. Treat Yourself Like a Dog—Celebrate All Wins
2. Focus on Progress First
3. Notice What is Going Right—The Satisfaction Mind Flip

There are reams of scientific evidence for the effectiveness of these three tools in building high-performing teams and in being a more effective parent and a happier, more fulfilled, and joyful person. In organizational development, this is called "Appreciative Inquiry." In parenting, it is called "catch your kids doing something right." I encourage you to take out this head trash and instill a new habit of noticing and celebrating all wins. You and everyone around you will appreciate it.

TAKE OUT THE HEAD TRASH SUMMARY

1. Deal with your inner critic.
2. Realize burnout is not a problem—it is a dilemma. Focus on building a strategy for balance.
3. Do the BIG 180–focus on what you want, not what you don't want.
4. Release the superhero—spin plates instead.
5. Celebrate all wins.

Take out the head trash ACTION STEPS

- What are the common things your inner critic says to slow you down?
- How does the distinction between a problem and a dilemma show up in other areas of your life?
- Make a list of the things that are going right in your life at this present moment.
- Where could you make more progress by spinning a plate and focusing on doing a good job with just one thing in your practice or life?
- What progress have you made toward a recent goal?

- How would you like to celebrate it? (A fist pump right now is probably a good start.)
- When will you do that?
- Journal on these questions.

CHAPTER 3

YOUR IDEAL PRACTICE

Building Your Blueprint and Master Plan for Change

"We are called to be architects of the future, not its victims."
—Buckminster Fuller

"When I'm working on a problem, I never think about beauty.
I only think about how to solve the problem. But, when I have finished,
if the solution is not beautiful, I know it is wrong."
—Buckminster Fuller

When you recognize your own dissatisfaction or burnout and use it to make changes in your practice, you can aim high or you can aim low. Most people aim low. When you are in survival mode, all you can focus on is something to ease your stress levels and treat or prevent symptomatic burnout. Better is good enough and probably all you are hoping for. That is aiming low.

I encourage you to aim higher

The tools in the remainder of this book can be used to accomplish all of those basic goals. You can lower your stress and treat or prevent burnout with every tool from here on out. They work when applied to that purpose.

If you aim higher, they can also be used to reach the ultimate goal—building your Ideal Practice and a rich and fulfilling life.

This is another example where you can rise above your physician programming. You have the ability to do the BIG 180 shift in your awareness here, too. You can move away from simple problem solving and focus on what you really want. That will seem a little foreign at first, I am sure. I encourage you to do it anyway.

It is not uncommon for me to ask overstressed doctors what they really want their practice to look like in an ideal world and be met with a slack-jawed, blank stare. The reply is generally along the lines of, "I don't know. No one has ever asked me that question."

That's because no one else has ever cared. As long as you are a train on someone else's tracks, all they care about is you doing their bidding. You are fulfilling their agenda. What you want has never been a consideration. Your desires are of no concern to your medical school, residency program, or your employer.

At the same time, you have always had wiggle room in your practice to shift things more toward what you really want. You just weren't aware of it until now. Check your aim here and let's shoot for the bull's-eye of your Ideal Practice rather than just some minor stress relief. Are you ready?

YOUR BLUEPRINT FOR CHANGE: THE IDEAL PRACTICE DESCRIPTION

You don't get what you want in life. You get what you tolerate.
—Anurag Gupta

THE FIRST STEP in creating your Ideal Practice is simple: build your Ideal Practice Description (IPD). Your IPD is your ultimate goal, your vision, the bull's-eye in your target. It is something you can run toward and allow to pull you forward, rather than continuously running away from the things you don't want.

KEYS TO CREATING A POWERFUL IDEAL PRACTICE DESCRIPTION

Write it down

I am old-school here, and I admit it. I encourage you to get a manila folder and label it "My Ideal Practice Description."

Use your favorite pen to write down the description of your Ideal Practice—your dream job—and keep this description in the manila folder. I love taking out that folder on a quiet Sunday morning and updating it. If you are more comfortable with a tablet computer and an electronic document, go that direction. The important thing here is that you have a fully fleshed-out Ideal Practice Description to organize your next steps.

Your Ideal Practice Description answers these questions:

If you had a magic wand and could wave it to pop your Ideal Practice into existence right here in front of you …
- What kinds of patients do you want to see?
  - What different kinds of people?
  - What diagnoses?
  - What procedures?
- In what setting?

- ➤ Office, hospital, both, multiple sites, or just one?
- ➤ Just you in the office/hospital, multiple doctors on site, physicians and PA's/NP's, in teams, or each with your own individual practice?
- For how many hours in the week and on what schedule?
- For what pay?
  - ➤ Insurance paid, cash payments, a mix, salary, or production, or both?
  - ➤ What is the minimum pay you must receive each month to support your family and your lifestyle?
- In what kind of a group?
  - ➤ Solo, physician-owned group, employee of large organization, academic practice, FQHC, profit, or non-profit?
- Of what size?
- With what kind of a group culture?
- How would you describe your ideal boss and his or her communication and leadership style?
- How does this group make decisions?
- Where do you want this practice to be located?
- In an urban or rural setting?
- In what area of the country or the world?
- With what recreational activities available to you?

It is your magic wand. Wave it. Imagine your Ideal Practice. Write it all down. Don't leave something off the list if a little voice is telling you it is impossible. Say, *thank you for sharing*, and write it down anyway. Your Ideal Practice is something to aspire to, so put it all down here.

DO NOT SKIP THIS STEP.

- Your Ideal Practice Description is unique to you.
- It is the *blueprint* to actually building your Ideal Practice.
- It creates a specific framework to focus all your efforts going forward.

Your clarity here on what you really want organizes all the steps that follow. Be patient and give yourself time to get clear on your own personal Ideal Practice Description now.

Imagine, for a second, trying to build a house without a blueprint. You may have been doing exactly that up until now with your career. You cobble together what seems to make sense at the time and find yourself doing the same things ten years later. Now, you pick your head up and realize—when you compare your current situation to your ideal—this practice didn't make sense then and makes even less sense now. Sound familiar?

<u>DO NOT SKIP THIS STEP: Without your Ideal Practice Description, you have no blueprint.</u>

You don't know where you are headed, *and* you cannot complete the next step: creating the *Master Plan* for this building project.

THREE THINGS TO KNOW ABOUT YOUR IDEAL PRACTICE DESCRIPTION

1. Getting clear on your Ideal Practice is a process.

This is a process. It takes time.

It normally takes a period of days to weeks to get clear on what you really want in your Ideal Practice. No one has ever asked you these questions before. It takes a while to recognize your programming and allow your dreams to wake up. Here's what I mean.

At some point back in your training, you had a dream of what it would be like to be a practicing physician. Take a second right now to think back on that dream. Now, look around at your current reality. You probably notice that old dream and your current reality don't overlap as well as you would like.

That dream has been asleep for a while. You were never taught how to use it as a blueprint. You were never taught the steps to actually bring it to life. There may even be a piece of you that has given up on the dream entirely.

It takes a while to wake your dream up, wipe off the guilt that sometimes tarnishes its surface these years later, and write it down.

Be patient with yourself. Keep picking up the folder, taking out your IPD, and adding and subtracting as things pop into your mind.

Along the way, there may be a little voice in your head saying things like, *What makes you think you are so special?* or, *Nobody gets everything they want; you should be satisfied with what you have.*

Do you recognize that as your inner critic?

You can tell these voices, *thank you for sharing*, and keep building your Ideal Practice Description. It is your programming speaking. Now, it is your turn to decide consciously what your Ideal Practice and life is and start living with purpose.

You Deserve This

Understand very clearly:

- You deserve this.
- You have earned it.
- Now is your time.

Creating your Ideal Practice Description is the first step in the process of living the dreams you held so hopefully way back at the beginning.

If You are Just Starting Out

If you are currently a medical student, resident, or in your first few years of practice, the Ideal Practice Description is even more important. Write down that dream *now* so you can maintain your focus and bring it to life ASAP.

2. Your Ideal Practice is a moving target.

Your Ideal Practice Description is not a static list of requirements. It is always changing, sometimes gradually and sometimes with stunning speed.

- Your IPD when you are single is different than when you have children.
- Your IPD is different when you are fifty-five than when you are thirty-five.
- Your IPD is different again when your kids are all grown and moved out.

What you feel to be your Ideal Practice may change dramatically overnight if a parent becomes ill and must move in with you, or any one of hundreds of similar life-altering events take place.

No matter what your age and situation, clarity on your IPD is a critical piece of your burnout prevention strategy and a key to actually building your Ideal Practice. You must review and tweak it regularly.

How often should you update your IPD?

From now on, make sure you update your IPD at least quarterly at a bare minimum—monthly is even better. Take the papers out, use a different color pen, and add and subtract as necessary.

3. Your Ideal Practice is an ideal.

Your IPD is something to aspire to. Realize almost no one will have a job that perfectly matches his or her ideal. So, if there is something you want to put on your Ideal Practice Description that is either difficult or impossible to achieve, put it in there anyway. Don't let the sarcastic voice of *Like that will ever happen!* stop you.

> ## Power Tip:
> **If you are comfortable with building a vision board,**
> **your IPD is a perfect place to put one into play.**

Example: My Ideal Life Story

You can expand this process to create your Ideal Life as well. It all starts with doing the BIG 180 and getting clear on what you really want.

When I was newly graduated from my residency, looking for a location to settle down and raise our family, my wife and I used this very same process without knowing it. Each of us wrote down the things we wanted in the ideal location, even if they seemed impossible.

- **Her list:** Small town within an hour's drive of a large city and a four-year university.
- **My list:** River running through the town with all five species of salmon in it, a rugby team, a full-spectrum family practice job, and two acres of bottom land.
- **On both lists:** Mountains and ocean side-by-side—as close as possible—and an old farmhouse in the country.

We ended up moving to Mount Vernon, Washington, in the Pacific Northwest and raising our two children—Rose and Sam—in a farmhouse built in 1907 on two acres of some of the richest river bottom soil in the world. Mountains—check. Ocean—check. Rugby team, river with all five species of salmon, Seattle and Western Washington University both less than an hour's drive away—check, check, check, and check. All those boxes were checked even though when we made that list we didn't think it was possible.

If there is something you want in your practice or your life, I encourage you to put it on your Ideal Practice Description and focus on finding it. Your clarity is power.

BUILDING THE PHYSICIAN'S VENN OF HAPPINESS

ONCE YOU HAVE your Ideal Practice Description in hand, you can build the following Venn diagram to help you bring it to life. I call this the "Physician's Venn of Happiness," because it will show you the shortest path from where you are now to a more Ideal Practice.

This simple diagram gives you power and precision you have not possessed until now.

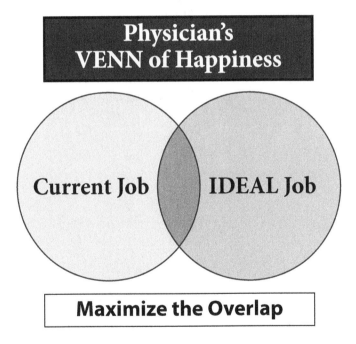

What is your current overlap?

When you are clear on your Ideal Practice Description, take a look at the Venn of Happiness above. Notice how much overlap it feels you have between your current practice and your IPD. This is a feeling more than a calculation. Write it down as a percentage.

Example:

It feels like there is about a 35 percent overlap between this practice and my Ideal Practice.

When I am working with a physician who is well into the downward spiral of burnout, they will tell me the overlap is in the 15-25 percent range.

Most physicians are very satisfied with their current job when the overlap is in the 75-80 percent and above range.

Your professional goal is to maximize the overlap.

The Venn of Happiness gives you the power to move in the direction of your Ideal Practice more quickly than you might imagine possible.

All you have to do is answer a supremely simple question to create the Master Plan for building your Ideal Practice.

THE MASTER PLAN QUESTION

WHAT WOULD YOU change about this job to increase the overlap with your Ideal Practice?

Normally when I ask this question to a client, a list of three to seven key changes comes flying out in rapid sequence.

Write these changes down.

Make a list of your answers to that question. Write down as many changes as you can think of—even if you think they are impossible.

This list is your Master Plan for building your Ideal Practice.

This is the master list of improvement projects for your practice. Keep them with your written Ideal Practice Description. Each time you make progress on even one of the changes on your list, you increase the overlap in the Venn of Happiness, automatically lower your stress levels, and build a more Ideal Practice.

Every single physician's Master Plan is as unique as your fingerprints.

This list and your Ideal Practice Description are a customized, highly specific plan you can follow to treat and prevent burnout. If you aim high enough, they will also help you build your Ideal Practice and a much more balanced life.

Use your Master Plan to select your tools.

A carpenter has to look at the blueprint to select the appropriate tools and materials he will take to the job site on any given day. The same principle applies for you in this Ideal Practice construction project. Use your Master Plan to decide which of the tools in chapter four are most appropriate for you.

Use your Master Plan to select your action steps.

With your Master Plan and appropriate tools in hand, you can focus like a laser on taking the most powerful actions. You can increase the overlap on your Venn of Happiness rapidly as you spin these plates of focused action one at a time.

Before you proceed further, take these two steps now:

1. Take at least a first pass on your Ideal Practice Description.

2. Take at least a first pass on your Master Plan to increase the overlap in the Venn of Happiness.

If you need to, put this book down, grab a pen and your favorite beverage, and do that now.

TWO WARNINGS

1. One Step at a Time

As doctors, we have a finely-tuned sense of urgency. One large danger to your progress here is to bite off more than you can chew right at the start.

You may be very excited at this point. You have your Ideal Practice Description and Master Plan in hand. You can probably visualize some clear steps to align that Venn diagram. Before you jump right in . . .

Remember plate spinning.

The temptation is to try to change a bunch of things at once. Don't do it. Remember, you are already busy to the point of overload. Recall the concept of plate spinning for a moment. One plate at a time …right?

Here is a way to take your list of changes and make progress without risking overload.

Look at your Master List of the changes you want to make.

- Prioritize them and *pick just one*. You may be a person who picks the biggest change first or someone who picks the easiest to start with. I recommend going with the easiest, simplest, and quickest change first. You are making changes *and* building your change-making muscles here. I encourage you to tackle a simple project first. Harvest the low hanging fruit and build your skills before you take on a bigger project that demands more of you and your team.
- Review the tools in chapter four and see which one best fits your needs.
- Then, plan your action step.
- What is the simplest thing you can do—the smallest first step—to put that change in action?
- When are you going to get it done?
- Get out your calendar and schedule it.
- Do it.

- Celebrate—actually pump your fist and say "*Yes,*" or give yourself a pat on the back. Treat yourself like a dog and celebrate all wins from this point forward.
- Once the first change is complete and you have this plate spinning nice and fast, take a look at your list and get started on the next thing.
- Journal on your experience on several different levels:
  - What was the change you made and what difference do you notice now?
  - What was your experience of consciously changing your practice to build a more satisfying work experience?
  - What did you learn?
  - What will you do differently as you make your next practice change?

2. Beware of Magical Thinking

Notice what comes up in your head the first time you look at the Venn of Happiness and ask the Master Plan question: *What would I change about this job to increase the overlap with my Ideal Practice?*

If a little voice in your head says something sarcastic like, "Get rid of EMR," I encourage you to notice that is magical thinking. EMR is not going away. We both know that is true, right?

It is okay and normal to have those thoughts; however, your Master Plan is better served by taking out that head trash and substituting a statement you can work with. Something like:

- Spend less time on documentation.
- Always have my charting done when I leave the office—and leave by 6 p.m.

As you work on this Master Plan item, you can see there are any number of ways to reach that goal, whereas, "Get rid of EMR" is magical thinking that just keeps you stuck in resentment and burnout.

BUILDING YOUR IDEAL PRACTICE SUMMARY

1. Create your Ideal Practice Description
2. Build the Physicians Venn of Happiness
3. Ask the following question to create your Master Plan: "*What would you change about this job to increase the overlap with your Ideal Practice?*"
4. Write down your list of answers. This is your Master Plan.

Building your Ideal Practice ACTION STEPS

- Create a folder (real or electronic) to store these core documents. Label it "My Ideal Practice Description"
- Take a first pass at your Ideal Practice Description.
  - ‣ Use colored pens, have some fun
  - ‣ Keep it in your folder
- Use the Venn of Happiness Diagram to estimate your current overlap in percent. Write that percentage down. This is your starting point.
- Ask, "What would you change about this job to increase the overlap with your Ideal Practice?"
- Label a document with "Master List" and write down all your answers. Keep this in your folder, too.
- Bring this folder, the IPD, and Master List to each of your weekly Strategy Sessions (see next chapter).
- Great work …Now, treat yourself like a dog.
  - ‣ You have laid the groundwork to create your ideal practice on purpose.
  - ‣ Pump your fist and say "YES" like you mean it.
  - ‣ Pat yourself on the back.
  - ‣ You now have your completely customized BLUEPRINT and MASTER PLAN in hand.
- In the chapters ahead, use these documents to choose the tools for your Ideal Practice building strategy.
- Commit to reviewing and updating these documents a minimum of quarterly—monthly, if possible.
- Journal on your experience.

CHAPTER 4

THE TOOLS

Field-Tested Tools to Prevent Burnout and Build Your Ideal Practice

"If you only have a hammer,
you tend to see every problem as a nail."
—Abraham Maslow

"No sooner do we think we have assembled a comfortable life
than we find a piece of ourselves that has no place to fit in."
—Gail Sheehy

"Life begins at the end of your comfort zone."
—Neale Donald Walsch

<u>Here we go: the tools section. Let's review what we have covered so far.</u>

- You understand burnout's symptoms, causes, effects, pathophysiology, and complications.
- You know burnout's highest and best use.
- You have liberated yourself from several pounds of head trash.
- You understand burnout is a dilemma not a problem, and we are focused on building a multi-part strategy to address it.
- You have a journal where you are reflecting on the ways all this new learning shows up in your life.
- You have a folder labeled "My Ideal Practice Description"—either hard copy or in an electronic format. Inside is your first pass at a description of your Ideal Practice.
- You understand the Physician's Venn of Happiness.
- You have your Master Plan list written down and in that folder as well. You have your initial list of practice changes that would align your practice more with your Ideal Practice.

Congratulations!

This is an enormous amount of progress given where you started. Take a breath or two now to congratulate yourself. I encourage you to reach your hand over one of your shoulders and give yourself a pat on the back. Treat yourself like a dog. You deserve it.

Power Tip:
**Give up the superhero and Lone Ranger right away.
Use your team instead.**

- I encourage you to recruit a support team for your transition. Share this book, your IPD, and your Master Plan with your spouse or significant other and your staff at work. You can pool your efforts to make the changes all of you would like to see. Sooner or later, you will be asking all of them to help you. Why not do that now, at the beginning of this process? Their help in brainstorming and sharing the action plan could make a huge difference right away.
- Consider assembling a study group of colleagues to work the steps together. You can support each other and build brainstorming and accountability partnerships to accelerate movement toward your Ideal Practice.

The four sections of this chapter hold a set of field-tested tools you can use to build your strategy for a more Ideal Practice. Along the way, you will also lower your stress levels, increase your ability to recharge, and prevent burnout.

Remember, burnout is a *dilemma*. You are building a *strategy* here.

There is no quick fix or single step that works like magic. This toolbox is a place where you can use your own Ideal Practice Description and Master Plan to pick and choose tools for your strategy and know they have been tested in the real world and proven effective.

Remember to spin plates. One tool at a time.

How do you choose which tools to use?

This process is a much like building a house. You have your Ideal Practice Description in hand, and you have used the Venn of Happiness to create your Master Plan of changes you would like to make. You already hold the Blueprint and Project List for this new "house" you are going to build.

- **Your Ideal Practice Description is the Blueprint for this new home.** It is your target. Everyone's Blueprint is unique. It is your responsibility to keep your Ideal Practice Description alive and up-to-date.
- **The Master Plan provides you with your Project List.** Here is the series of changes you must make to build the house in the blueprint. Just like a house plan has many components—wiring, plumbing, framing, flooring—your Project List will involve addressing the key elements that must change to build your Ideal Practice. You will probably build strategies to address job stresses, work-life balance, EMR, and other issues. Everyone's Ideal Practice Master List is unique. It is your responsibility to use the Venn of Happiness to create and prioritize your Master Plan.
- **The individual tools you are about to learn are the bricks and mortar, lumber and nails, for this building project.** These are the basic building blocks of new awareness and new actions needed to build your Ideal Practice.

Before we get to the actual tools, let me give you a suggestion on how to start and nurture this project, as well as a framework for understanding the tools that follow.

COMMIT TO REGULAR STRATEGY SESSIONS

MOST PHYSICIANS I work with didn't burnout yesterday, recognize it immediately, and then call me for a Discovery Session today. Burnout is not something you recognize right away. This is one of the classic "frog in a pot" situations where you don't notice the problem until it has been around for a long time.

We get too busy dealing with the sheer volume of activities required to run our practices and our lives that we lose all perspective. We are too busy to pick our heads up and notice what is going on, much less change things around us.

You must work *ON* your practice, not just *IN* it.

In order to make the changes you want, you must set aside time to step out of your routine, look down on your life, and practice from a strategic perspective. Only when you step out of the flow of your current habits can you build an effective strategy and ask important questions like:

- What is it I really want?
- How are things going so far?
- What is working and what is not?
- What do I want to change?
- When will I take the first step?

How much time will you need?

I suggest you devote a minimum of one hour every other week to your own personal strategy session. This is the *minimum* amount to create momentum toward your Ideal Practice you will be able to feel. If you want to move faster, schedule one hour *each* week.

Suggested Strategy Session agenda:

1. Get out your Ideal Practice Description and Master Plan.
2. Have pen and paper or an open word processing document at hand for notes and ideas.
3. Review and update your Ideal Practice Description.
4. Review the Venn of Happiness and your Master Plan.

5. Review progress on your action steps from last week. Celebrate all wins and effort from last week.

6. Use your Master Plan to prioritize and study one tool in this book. The ACTION STEP list following each tool will guide your study and the translation of your new knowledge into meaningful actions.

7. Schedule your action steps for the week ahead.

   • What Master Plan project are you addressing now? What action comes next?

   • What ACTION STEP for which tool would you like to take in this coming week? You may be practicing the same tool week-to-week or picking up a new one. What is this week's step?

8. Schedule your next Strategy Session. This Strategy Session is not complete until your next one is on your calendar.

THE BURNOUT PREVENTION MATRIX: ORIENTATION TO THE TOOLS

LET'S RECALL THE simple energetic rules that govern burnout.

- Burnout is caused by stress.
  - ‣ Stress drains your energy accounts (physical, emotional, and spiritual).
  - ‣ If you are unable to recharge your energy accounts, they will eventually fall to a negative balance.
  - ‣ When your energy accounts fall into negative balance, burnout symptoms kick in.
  - ‣ "You can't give what you ain't got."
- The four sources of stress and causes of burnout are:
  - ‣ The practice of medicine
  - ‣ Your job
  - ‣ Having a life
  - ‣ Your programming

The Two Methods to Prevent Burnout

1. Lower your stress levels and the drain they cause.
2. Increase your ability to recharge your energy accounts.

The Two Responsible Parties in Our Prevention Efforts:

1. The individual physician—that would be you.
2. Your organization—the entity that is responsible for the workplace conditions of your current job.

Put these together, and you create a classic 2X2 matrix that will organize the tools in this chapter.

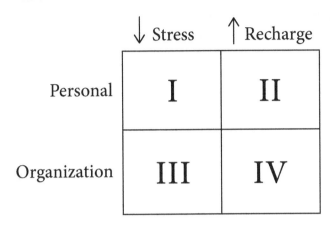

The Burnout Prevention Matrix

	↓ Stress	↑ Recharge
Personal	I	II
Organization	III	IV

<u>**In this chapter, you will learn several of the most powerful matrix tools in detail.**</u>

All of the tools are field-tested and doctor-approved through my own life and the lives and practices of hundreds of my one-on-one physician coaching clients. They are a selection of the first and most powerful burnout prevention techniques I teach.

<u>**Our focus will be on the things for which you can take complete responsibility.**</u>

These are new levels of awareness and new activities that you can put into place on your own. None of them require the approval of your supervisor, a budget, or the assistance of your IT department—thank heavens.

<u>**I suggest you read through the rest of this chapter as an overview first.**</u>

- Look at all the tools from each of the four quadrants.
- Take notes in your journal.
- Notice which tools fit into your Master Plan of changes you want to make to your current practice.
- Read and follow the ACTION STEPS for your selected tools at the end of their sections to start practicing them.
- Get ready to spin up your first plate in your next strategy session.

One Last Bit of Head Trash to Take Out

Before you move on to the tools, we have one more piece of head trash to isolate and remove.

You are going to be learning and practicing new skills in the pages ahead. You are a beginner here, and there is an important first lesson to learn.

Complete the following statement:

"Practice makes [_____]."

If you answered with the word "perfect," I want you to know that is a piece of head trash. There is a place in everyone's awareness that says, *I will never be perfect, so why practice?*

"Practice makes perfect" is actually a non-supportive thought. It comes from your perfectionist programming, and it will block your impulse to do the work of practicing any new skill. Yet, practice is absolutely essential for a simple reason:

Practice makes *BETTER.*

Remember this when you are practicing the new skills below. Remember it when you are helping your patients, staff, or family members learn new skills.

Practice makes better.

Practice with this mindset. Learn to live your life from this new perspective and see what a difference it makes.

Fill in the blank:

Practice Makes [_____]

QUADRANT I: PERSONAL STRESS RELIEF

*"A real decision is measured by the fact that you've taken a new action.
If there's no action, you haven't truly decided."*
—Tony Robbins

*"Many of us feel stress and get overwhelmed not because we're taking on too much, but
because we're taking on too little of what really strengthens us."*
—Marcus Buckingham

ELECTRONIC MEDICAL RECORDS (EMR) AND DOCUMENTATION

IN EVERY SURVEY of physician stress factors, EMR tops the list. The hassles of documentation can get in the way of being present with the patient and block you from any semblance of a healing patient encounter. It is not uncommon for physicians to spend hours after their last patient typing in the EMR and additional hours at home with documentation after the kids are in bed.

EMR is also the most common aspect of clinical practice where physicians feel out of control and victimized, wish for a magic pill solution, or wish that EMR would just go away.

These symptoms among physicians should be a head trash clue for you at this point. As you read this sentence, imagine a flashing red light leaping from the page and a claxon screaming, "DILEMMA ALERT ...DILEMMA ALERT..."

Remember our discussion of problems vs. dilemmas back in chapter two?

<u>EMR is not a problem. EMR is another dilemma.</u>

Much of physician's suffering around EMR is because it is not a problem, no matter how much we would like it to be. Before I help you shape your strategy to address EMR, here are the most important things to know about it.

EMR is not going away—no matter how much you might wish it would. It is here to stay. You either learn to be as much of an expert in the software as you can—or build a team that is expert in its use—or you will suffer and get home later than needed.

There is no "solution" for EMR and the requirements of documentation. This is not because it is impossible to solve. It is because EMR is *not a problem*. You can stop trying to solve it or wishing it would disappear.

EMR is a true blue dilemma.

If you want to minimize its effect on your quality of life and get home sooner, your job is to:

1. **DEFINE** the two horns of the dilemma and the optimum balance point.
2. Design a **STRATEGY** to create the balance you seek.
3. Build a **SYSTEM** to monitor the effectiveness of your strategy.
4. **TWEAK** your strategy and your system as often as you need to.

The Two Horns

I believe the best expression of the two horns of the EMR dilemma is *Documentation vs. Effort (time and energy)*. The balance point you seek is adequate documentation with the minimum input of effort.

Let me show you a suggested EMR strategy and a system for tracking its effectiveness here. It is up to you to pick a piece of the strategy and put it to use. Remember plate spinning and the one-at-a-time method of implementation of your action steps. Remember, too, that this is a strategy. It will ultimately have multiple parts.

A Suggested EMR Strategy

1. Check Your Attitude

One of the biggest problems with EMR is our attitude toward the technology. We treat the computer and the documentation programs as if they rose from the very fires of hell to torment us. You will recognize complaining and blaming as signs you are playing the role of the victim. Remember, this is just head trash.

When we fail to embrace the technology, we never learn how to use it well. Every time you touch the keyboard, your attitude changes and hassles seem to sprout like weeds in a garden.

Don't be a hater.

Hating the EMR is an emotion that gets in the way of completing your documentation efficiently.

Here is a place where I am very sympathetic with your situation. I understand how painful it can be to stop seeing patients at five, do two more hours of charting at the office, head home and eat dinner at seven thirty, put the kids to bed, and spend two more hours of charting on your home computer—and still you are not done. It is painful, exhausting, frustrating, maddening, and more.

My sympathy, empathy, and compassion does absolutely no good unless—and until—you step away from playing the victim. Victims don't get better at documentation. Victims blame, justify, and complain while nothing around them changes.

EMR is here to stay. If you don't embrace it and learn to be an expert at it, you are only guaranteeing your misery and struggles will continue.

There are ways to improve your skills, set up better-shared documentation tasks, and use your team more efficiently. Check your attitude and take the step below.

2. Commit to Becoming a Power User

I encourage you to commit to becoming a power user of your specific EMR system. Do everything you can to become an expert in the documentation program in your office. Here are some steps that work in the real world.

a) Take all the training your vendor gives you—twice.

Make sure your nurses and receptionists do, too. Learn everything there is to learn from the vendor's trainings, and realize that is just a basic foundation.

b) Use the full capabilities of the software.

Believe it or not, EMR programs were designed with the intention to make documentation easier. Unfortunately, most were not designed by working doctors. However, all of them have features that allow you to perform automated entry of chart notes in the form of templates and other methods of chunking in content you would normally have to free type in over and over again.

As a power user, you will want to develop every single ounce of the customization options for your software so that it matches your personal practice.

Here is the acid test for your documentation. Answer this question:

If you look back over a week's chart notes, what percentage of the data entry do you *free type* into the chart?

You are doing very well if your answer is 30 percent or less. If you find yourself free typing most of every chart note, there are massive time savings available to you from using the automation functions inside your software.

- Templates
- Quick keys
- Any type of templated automatic entry within the system's capability

Take the time to match as much automation as you can to the diagnoses, procedures, and patient encounters you see the most in your practice. Any time you find yourself doing the same keystrokes or typing out mouse patterns, it is a cry to customize that piece of your EMR to automate that sequence.

Remember the 80–20 rule. 20 percent of your diagnoses account for 80 percent of your documentation volume. Develop your templates one at a time with that in mind.

c) Study the Native Power Users in Your Group

- Who are the people in your practice that do not complain about the EMR?
- Who are the doctors/nurses/receptionists that get home on time with their work done and love the program—the ones everyone acknowledges are good at it, the ones who would never go back to your old charting method?
- NOTE: These power users may be in hiding in your organization. It is often not popular to like EMR. You may have to dig a little to find them.

Ask them if you can watch how they chart.

They always say, "Yes." Arrange a time when you can sit next to them while they are at their computer. Sit just over their shoulder and lean in the way an umpire in the major leagues leans on the back of the catcher. Watch exactly what they do when they are charting. If that means you accompany them into the exam room, so be it.

There will come a moment when you suddenly tell them to stop as they do a quick set of keystrokes, completing a patient note in a millisecond. Stop them whenever you need them to stop. Don't ask them what their favorite shortcuts are. You probably wouldn't understand their explanation. Instead, have them show you *exactly* what they do when they are charting. Take notes. Learn their shortcuts by watching what they do in their practice.

Ask to borrow their templates for diagnoses you both share.

These are the people who have the most useful templates covering the most diagnoses of anyone in your group. They are always just fine with sharing. It is no work on their part to export their templates to your computer. In fact, I have never heard of a power user refusing this request.

Now that you have watched them working the EMR and have their templates, do what they do, the way they do it, and keep tweaking this foundation to match your practice even more effectively.

Just one tip from a power user colleague can make a huge difference in each patient encounter when you are back in your office. Saving a couple minutes on every patient with a URI from this day forward will eventually add up to major time savings for you.

Pick one diagnosis or procedure, create and deploy a template, and see how it works for you. Then, pick another each week until your most common visits are template. Remember, you only have to create a template once. You benefit from that template forever.

3. Chart only what is required—the minimum data set.

Last but not least, it is very important to recognize and release your perfectionist programming. Most physicians who really struggle with charting are being driven by their perfectionist programming to write the ideal note every time. I strongly encourage you to stop that now.

A chart note is not the Great American Novel.

Punctuation, sentence structure, and grammar are irrelevant. Ask yourself, *What are the purposes of a chart note?* Document only enough to fulfill those purposes. Here are the three purposes of a chart note. They form the boundaries of the smallest and most efficient note you can enter into your EMR.

The Three Purposes of a Chart Note

- **Continuity of Care.** Looking at your chart note, the reader (you or another provider) should be able to orient themselves to the symptoms, diagnosis, your thought process, and treatment plan. Full sentences are an obstruction to clarity here. Bullets are a more effective way to bring the reader up to speed. Punctuation is irrelevant. Minor misspellings are of no consequence. The question to ask is, "Does this note orient the reader to the illness and my treatment plan quickly and efficiently?"
- **Billing.** Most EMR programs are set up to document at a level that justifies your billing charge automatically. Usually, you can even check a level higher than you are used to charging and the support will be there. Documentation for billing is much less of a concern with EMR than in the days of paper charts and is probably not driving your urge to write too much.
- **Covering Your "Legal Part."** All of us subconsciously document in a way that

would protect us if this patient were to sue. Do what you have to and not a semicolon more here.

This concept of documenting the minimum adequate data set underlies all of the other recommendations above. It is something to keep in mind at all times.

4. Use Your Team

Once you are on your path to becoming a power user, don't forget you have a team here. I encourage you to rise above your Lone Ranger programming and utilize all the brainstorming power of your patient care team. Gather your receptionist and nurse (or anyone who is involved in your patient flow or chart entries before and after you see them), and get everyone's ideas on how to share the tasks of charting.

This involves you stepping out of the traditional doctor leadership paradigm as the person with all the answers who "gives orders" to the team. Here, you are asking powerful, open-ended questions that start with the words *what* or *how*. Here are some examples:

- What do you see me doing that I can stop—or you can do better?
- What ideas do you have on how we can make documentation easier?
- How can we share the charting activities more effectively?

In most cases, your team has important ideas they have not shared with you, because you have not given them the green light in this way.

Make a list of their ideas, prioritize the suggestions, and pick one to implement. Get that plate spinning nice and fast and that team documentation step to the point of being a solid habit before you choose and implement team documentation step number two.

5. Consider Negotiating for a Scribe

The keys to getting a scribe if you are employed by a large organization are always money, manpower, and your skills at negotiation. Most doctors go about their attempts to get a scribe in ways that guarantee they will be turned down.

Don't Do This

You can't just walk into an administrator's office, rant about how the EMR is an abomination, and demand a scribe. Lots of doctors do exactly that. Sometimes, you can hear them blame and complain all the way down the hall.

Here is what typically happens. The administrator you have just backed into the corner will say something like, "...and just who is going to pay for that?" or "If I give you one, then everybody will want one," and turn you down flat.

If you really want a scribe and you meet resistance from your group, the biggest question is this: *Are you willing to pay for it out of your salary (at least to start the project)?*

If you are the first person in your practice to get one, you will most likely need to pay for a scribe yourself until you can document that the two of you are able to see more patients and create more income than you alone.

NOTE: Remember to plan for the situation where your scribe is sick and you have to do the charting that day. You don't want your practice to grind to a complete halt on any day your scribe can't make it in. It is lower risk to hire a pair of part-time scribes and build some redundancy into your staffing from the start. They can cover for each other and dramatically decrease the days when you are on your own.

Track productivity to set up the claw back.

Make sure your group tracks your productivity before and after the scribe. If there is an increase in your collections with the scribes that is equal to or greater than their salary, you may be able to negotiate for the group to pay their salary in the future. Make sure that you have the pre- and post-scribe data to do that analysis.

An EMR Strategy Monitoring System

Here are some metrics I suggest you consider using to monitor the effectiveness of your EMR strategy:

- The average amount of time between seeing your last patient and leaving the office or hospital.
- The number of incomplete charts outstanding. Zero is best, and you will probably have a few now and then no matter what. Tell your perfectionist programming to give you a break when this happens.
- The amount of time you spend charting from home. Again, you may need to do this from time to time no matter what. Perfectionist be gone!

EMR/DOCUMENTATION SUMMARY

1. EMR is a dilemma.
2. You are looking to build an EMR strategy.
3. Suggested EMR strategy steps
   - Don't be a hater
   - Become a power user
   - Chart the minimum data set
   - Use your team
   - Negotiate for a scribe

EMR/Documentation ACTION STEPS

NOTE: The plate spinning theory applies here. These are components of an EMR strategy that will work. Implement them one at a time.

- Check your attitude when using the EMR. Consider giving up any negative thoughts or feelings to the Squeegee Breath (which we'll discuss in the next section) so they don't slow you down.
- Consider using one of the steps in your charting routine as a trigger for your Squeegee Breath. (See "Mindfulness-Based Stress Relief (MBSR) and the Squeegee Breath" in the next section.)
- Take a look at your current chart notes. How can you trim them down to the minimum notes required?
- When can you request and review the training available for your EMR system?
- Who are the native power users in your group? If you are in a solo practice, ask your EMR vendor who else is using your EMR system to find the power users in your town.
- When will you schedule a power user observation session?
- Ask your team how they recommend you divvy up documentation responsibilities to increase your team's efficiency and save extra steps.
- Prioritize, select, and implement a team documentation activity.
- If you choose to negotiate for a scribe:
  - Find out their typical salary.
  - Make the decision to hire them in a pilot project with you paying their salary.

- ‣ Negotiate for them to be hired.
- ‣ Agree on how to track your combined productivity.
- ‣ Work to increase your patient volumes sufficiently enough to justify the scribe's salary and negotiate for the group to take that off your hands down the road.
- Journal on your experiences.

MINDFULNESS-BASED STRESS RELIEF (MBSR) AND THE SQUEEGEE BREATH

"Mindfulness is simply being aware of what is happening right now without wishing it were different; enjoying the pleasant without holding on when it changes (which it will); being with the unpleasant without fearing it will always be this way (which it won't)."
—James Baraz

"The best way to capture moments is to pay attention. This is how we cultivate mindfulness. Mindfulness means being awake. It means knowing what you are doing."
—Jon Kabat-Zinn

MINDFULNESS-BASED STRESS RELIEF teaches you how to monitor and optimize "who you are being" at work.

With an effective mindfulness practice, you can become the "eye of the storm" in your practice day—calm and centered no matter what is going on around you. This is not positive psychology or thinking happy thoughts. Mindfulness is a powerful, proven stress relief tool for physicians. It has a history of stress relieving effects that go back thousands of years.

Jon Kabat-Zinn

The use of mindfulness as a tool in healthcare in the US begins with Jon Kabat-Zinn and his founding of the Center for Mindfulness in Medicine, Health Care, and Society at the University of Massachusetts in 1979.

Kabat-Zinn was a student of the Vietnamese Buddhist monk Thích Nhất Hạnh, from whom he learned *vipassanā*, or mindfulness meditation. He originally taught meditation, simple yoga poses, and body scan imagery to patients in the UMass healthcare system with mental and physical diseases. Mindfulness was so effective in symptom relief across such a broad range of illnesses that soon the doctors began to attend classes alongside their patients.

The physicians noticed they learned to become calmer, more centered, and more focused in their practices as a result of learning to meditate. Multiple studies replicating Kabat-Zinn's program have shown significant stress relief effects for physicians in the last thirty years. Today, Mindfulness-Based Stress Relief (MBSR) is acknowledged as the most researched and effective burnout prevention tool for doctors.

What is mindfulness?

The simplest and most accurate description of the state of mindfulness is this: *being present to what is happening here and now; releasing thoughts and feelings that keep you from this present moment without judgment.*

Mindfulness means giving whatever is in front of you right now *your undivided attention.*

Here is why this is such a powerful stress relieving and illness modifying skill. Notice how often your mind wanders to topics that are not in front of you here and now, especially when you are in the flow of seeing patients in your practice.

It is extremely common for our thoughts to be dominated by:

- Worrying about things you did and patients you saw earlier in the day (the past).
- Thinking about things on your to-do list that you haven't gotten to yet—or patients you will be seeing later today (the future).
- Fear that something bad that happened in the past is going to happen again in the future (projection).
- Those funny random thoughts that come up in daydreams or distractions.

All of these thought patterns are normal, constant, and interfere with you giving *this* patient or *this* task your undivided attention in *this* moment. The distractions from being present are not just at work either. You are just as likely to be distracted when you are with your spouse or significant other or children when you are away from the office.

When your awareness is dominated by worrying about the past or future, you are not able to relax into the present. It is stressful, even though we often don't even realize it is going on. The distraction of our consciousness causes a near constant trickle of stress and energy leakage. Mindfulness can stop the worry and the drain distraction causes, allowing you to be present, focused, and relaxed as you address the task at hand.

<u>**Mindfulness is a skill set you use to:**</u>

- **NOTICE** you are not present—that your thoughts and feelings are distracted.
- **RELEASE** those thoughts and feelings without judging yourself for having them.
- **RETURN** your undivided attention to the present and the task at hand.

NOTICE > RELEASE > RETURN

<u>**Why is mindfulness important?**</u>

Your ability to be fully present and focus your undivided attention on the person or task in front of you is the key to a number of very important components of career and life satisfaction.

<u>**Mindfulness is a core skill of:**</u>

- Leadership
- Quality care and patient satisfaction—mindfulness is the essence of the healing encounter
- Parenting
- Love and caring for another
- Focus and attention to detail
- "Flow"—when you become completely absorbed in an activity to the point where time passes without you noticing
- Your ability to respond to an emergency situation such as a code

Mindfulness is such a foundational skill for the art of being a doctor, leader, spouse, and parent that I find it strange it is almost never taught to physicians until *after* they are suffering from burnout.

<u>**The fast track to mindfulness**</u>

Jon Kabat-Zinn taught meditation as a mindfulness tool, because that is how he learned it from Thích Nhất Hạnh. His training requires hours of weekly seated and walking meditation and a two-day silent meditation retreat as your graduation from the program. This significant time commitment is the biggest impediment to wide adoption by physicians. Most doctors feel they are just too busy to take the time to develop a formal meditation practice.

Since he started the Center for Mindfulness, most studies of MBSR simply copied his training with different participant groups. We won't be doing that here. It is important to realize that meditation is only one of many paths to practice mindfulness. It is the way a Buddhist monk learns and teaches, but it is not the only way to cultivate your undivided attention.

Another drawback to formal meditation practice as a mindfulness tool is its abstraction from the workplace. The term "formal meditation" means carving a specific time out of the normal routine of your day to meditate. Then, you sit in silence in a special environment with special cushions, far from the physical environment and stresses of your medical practice. You are practicing mindfulness in the absence of the stresses and distractions you hope it will help you address. Kabat-Zinn and other researchers have proven that meditation away from the workplace is effective in lowering stress, but why not start with a tool you can use when you need it most?

How about a mindfulness tool you can use inside the flow of your practice activities—something you can do at work to return to the present while you are hip deep in the distractions of your practice?

Enter the "Squeegee Breath"

In late 2013, the Multicare Health System in Tacoma, Washington worked with me to recruit twenty-four physician volunteers for a study of a single-breath mindfulness tool I call the "Squeegee Breath." Our goal was to prove a single breath at the point of care was as effective in lowering stress and preventing burnout as meditation-based mindfulness.

The Squeegee Breath is a four-part super-breath that can be incorporated seamlessly into any physician's practice. You can learn the technique in five minutes and begin to use and benefit from it immediately. You will be learning and using it in your practice here in just a minute or two.

In the study, we delivered eight weekly video lessons to our participants with weekly phone drop-in coaching support. We measured sixteen different scales of stress, burnout, and mindfulness at baseline, again at the end of the lessons, and a third time eight weeks after graduation. The study produced significant improvements in thirteen of the sixteen measurements that persisted to the eight weeks post-graduation survey point.

As I write this, we have submitted the study to several journals for publication and are awaiting their reply. This chapter contains an abbreviated version of lessons one and two of the eight lessons in the full training. In the pages below, you will learn the full Squeegee Breath technique and how to use a trigger to transform it into a daily habit in your practice.

This is the first burnout prevention tool I teach every one-on-one coaching client.

It is the key step to ending the downward spiral, because it is about who you are being. You can release the stress around you and use your ability to be present as a barrier to further energy loss. You don't need anyone else's approval or permission. You can get started with the Squeegee Breath immediately while we plan the changes in your practice that will take more time to implement.

You Can Do This

Before we begin, let me reassure you—you already know how to do this. The Squeegee Breath builds on what I call "native human mindfulness behavior."

Remember the last time you were standing in the hallway of your practice. The exam room door was closed in front of you and you knew "Mavis" was on the other side. There is a Mavis in every practice. She is the patient you know is going to be a handful, just like always. You have probably been thinking about her ever since you saw her name on the schedule earlier in the day. You take a look at the chart, and it's time to open the door and get started.

As you put your hand on the doorknob, you pause. What do you do before you enter the room?

Right. You take a deep breath.

Why?

Right again. You are centering yourself so you are fully present and ready for anything. After all, we are talking about Mavis here.

That is native human mindfulness behavior. In this example, you take the breath without being aware of your intention. The Squeegee Breath transforms this normal behavior into a four-part super-breath you use with the conscious intention of focusing your awareness in the present.

Why "Squeegee?"

Think about the way you experience your reality under normal circumstances. Your awareness, operating through your senses, creates a window to the outside world. When you are preoccupied by thoughts and feelings, the distraction interferes with your ability to be present. It is as if your window to the world has become smudged and cloudy. You can't even see what is right in front of you clearly. You need an awareness window washer. You need a squeegee.

Have you ever seen a professional window washer cleaning the big windows on storefronts in your town? They have a wand covered with soap and water in one hand. They use the wand to scrub the window. In the other hand they have a squeegee. With a single swipe of the squeegee, the window is squeaky clean, so clear it is difficult to see there is a pane of glass in front of you.

Let me show you how to use a "Squeegee Breath" to clean the window of your awareness, release any thoughts or feelings that don't need to be here right now, and become calm, centered, and present. This is a single breath method to give any object, person, or task your undivided attention.

The Squeegee Breath in Four Steps

Let's take a first walk through the four steps of the Squeegee Breath. Feel free to practice each step as you read it.

1. Intention

Set the intention that you are going to release anything that does not need to be here at this point in time and become calm, relaxed, and completely present.

2. Breathe In

Take a big breath in, all the way up to the top of your head.
Hold that breath in for a count of …two …three …

3. Breathe Out and Release

Release and exhale all the way to the bottom of your feet. As this out breath moves from your head to your toes, feel the squeegee passing down the window of your awareness. You can release any distracting or non-supportive thought to this cleansing breath. Let the squeegee wipe you clean.

As you reach the bottom of that breath, hold it out for a count of …two …three …

4. Smile

Let your breathing resume itself.

As you inhale, smile and say "ahh."

Now It's Your Turn

If you were just reading the words above on this first time through, it's time to practice. Remember Einstein's definition of insanity; you have to take different actions if you want different results in your life. Here is another chance to do just that. I encourage you to stand up for your first couple Squeegee Breaths so you really get that sense of being wiped clean on the exhale.

Please stand up.

1. **Intention:** Set your intention to release and become present.
2. **Breathe In:** Inhale to the top of your head. Hold it in…two…three…
3. **Breathe Out:** Exhale to the bottoms of your feet. Release. Give it all up to the squeegee. Hold it out…two…three…
4. **Smile:** Resume your normal breathing pattern. Smile. Say "ahh."

Feels good, doesn't it? Here's the thing about the Squeegee Breath.

It works every time you use it.

When I say it works, I mean you will be calmer, more relaxed, and more present after you take a Squeegee Breath than you were before.

I have taught this one breath mindfulness tool to hundreds of coaching clients and thousands of physicians in live trainings. I often hear from experienced meditators that it is more effective than the meditation they have done regularly for years. Here is why that is true for many.

How the Squeegee Breath Works

The four parts of the Squeegee Breath combine to give you an authentic super-breath. It is a highly concentrated mini-meditation.

- Your intention is the most important part. Your desire to release and become present—and your intention that this next breath will provide that experience for you—is key.
- Breathing from your head to your toes provides a full-body release. You will

get better and better at actually breathing from your head to your toes as you practice.

- The image of the squeegee wiping you clean allows you to feel the release as you exhale.
- Smiling and saying "ahh" is a mini-reward and celebration of you taking good care of yourself.

You Practice the Squeegee "In Situ"

Best of all, you do all this right in the middle of your workday, the exact time and place you need it the most. It is like taking a class in college where they give you the final exam on day one. Well, you just passed the final, and it all gets easier from here.

What to Give Up to the Squeegee Breath

Feel free to let go of any unsupportive or distracting thoughts. Anything that takes you away from what is in front of you right now is something you can give up to the squeegee.

You may have a little voice in your head saying something like, *This is pretty wild, Buddhist, tutti-fruitti, woo-woo, out there weirdness.* Or, your inner voice might be saying, *I hope I am doing it the right way.* If you want, you can let both of those thoughts go to the squeegee.

- Set your intention to let them go.
- Big breath to the top of your head…two…three…
- Release to the bottoms of your feet…two…three…
- Inhale. Smile. Say "ahh."

The Squeegee Breath is Like Kegel Exercises

You may also hear your inner voice say, *There is no way I am doing this in front of my patients and staff.* You can give that up, too.

Out in the real world, a Squeegee Breath is a lot like Kegel exercises. Someone would really have to be watching you closely to notice the change in your breathing, especially if you do it while you are washing your hands, walking down the hallway, or in the privacy of your office.

So, there you have it. A research-proven, single-breath mindfulness technique you can put to use and benefit from immediately. In fact, you probably already have. With the four parts of the Squeegee Breath, you are always only a single breath away from being much calmer, more centered, and more present.

NOTE: The only way you are too busy for the Squeegee is if you are too busy to breathe.

When to Take a Squeegee Breath

Let me green light you to do it PRN ...whenever you feel you need it. I only wish it was that easy. However, with physicians, waiting until you feel like you need to take a Squeegee Breath is always a spectacular failure for a simple reason: your conditioning.

You are highly conditioned to ignore your own stress, worry, and distraction levels. If you wait until you feel like you need the squeegee, it is nearly always too late.

The Squeegee Breath is most effective when it becomes a regular habit in your practice day. Here is a lesson in habit formation science from the Stanford Persuasive Technology Laboratory that will help you develop your own Squeegee Breath habit.

The head of the lab is a fascinating man named B.J. Fogg. He spends half his time researching how to motivate people to change their behavior and the other half working with the developers of cell phone applications to make them more addictive.

Let me teach you one of his core concepts. If you're interested in learning more about him and his work, his website is *www.bjfogg.com*.

Dr. Fogg says that to create a new habit, you need to possess three things at once.

1. Ability

You have to know how to do the new thing you want to do. In this case, you know how to do the Squeegee Breath. There are no more steps, no advanced training, and nothing more to learn about how to perform the Squeegee Breath. All that remains is for you to practice it. You have the ability now and will only get more skilled with time because Practice Makes _____.[9]

2. Motivation

I have to assume you are motivated to lower your stress levels and be more present with your patients, staff, and family. I assume you can see the benefits of being completely present with all three and giving them the benefit of your undivided attention. So, you have the motivation, too.

3. A Trigger

All that is missing right now is a trigger. This is just like a trigger on a gun. The trigger reminds you to take the action. You need a trigger to remind you to do the Squeegee Breath in your workday.

B.J. Fogg says the very best trigger is an existing habit. You trigger a new habit with an old one. See how this works?

Ideally, you choose a special type of existing habit he calls a Super Habit.

Super Habits are things you would never not do. The best Super Habits are also things you do repeatedly in the day. That way, you trigger the Squeegee Breath multiple times a day, whether you feel like you need it or not. This allows you to be proactive and get ahead of the stresses in your practice, rather than waiting to notice you are frustrated and distracted before taking action.

Now, here is one reason I love working with doctors—among many mind you. Answer this question for me:

What is something you do multiple times a day in the office—perhaps between each patient—that you would never not *do?*

Think about it for a few seconds, and you will see the routine of your patient flow has dozens of Super Habits embedded within. The most obvious one is hand washing. Others include opening the door, reviewing the chart, multiple different steps in the EMR you take with each patient, using the bathroom, sitting down in your office chair, and many more.

All you have to do is pick one. Then, set the intention that you will use this Super Habit as your Squeegee Breath trigger. Add in a simple way of tracking how often you take a Squeegee Breath in your day and you are nearly there.

I recommend you track your progress with a sticky note in a prominent place—one that you walk past regularly in your day. Put a pen or pencil tick mark every time you take a Squeegee Breath. Celebrate every one.

- Treat yourself like a dog.
- Keep track of your totals from day to day.
- Feel free to switch out your Super Habit trigger if you find this one difficult.
- Play with different triggers until you hit on one that works for you.

You are now a Squeegee Breath teacher, too.

You weren't aware until now that the last several pages were the Squeegee Breath train-the-trainer course as well. You are now also a fully-fledged Squeegee Breath trainer. I strongly encourage you to teach this single super-breath technique to your staff, your patients, and your family.

In our twenty-four-doctor study, the participants related multiple examples of how sharing a Squeegee Breath brought them closer to their patients. This was especially true with the patients who were most upset in their office that day. Here is an example of how you might do in your practice.

Sharing the Squeegee

Let's say you walk into the exam room and the patient is in pain or upset.

Notice it and say something like, "You look uncomfortable and upset. Let's take a big breath together and let some of that go."

Then look them in the eye and breathe "squeegee style" with them as many times as you would like. You will see them relax and synchronize their breathing with yours—and probably smile and thank you with each breath.

That is all it takes. You don't have to say the word squeegee if you don't want to. I guarantee the patient will appreciate your caring and feel better after the breaths.

The same breath works just as well with your staff and especially with your children. Remember, you are a certified Squeegee Breath instructor now. Spread the benefits of mindfulness by simply teaching people how to breathe with an intention.

For full video training on the Squeegee Breath, triggers, and the additional six modules of the complete 1-Minute Mindfulness Program we used in the physician's study, you will find a link in the Power Tools Library on the web here: *www.thehappymd.com/powertools*.

SQUEEGEE BREATH SUMMARY

1. Mindfulness is noticing you are distracted, releasing the distracting thoughts and feelings, and returning to give the present moment your *undivided attention*.
2. Squeegee Breath: Four Steps
   - Intention: Set your intention to release and become present.
   - Breathe In: Inhale to the top of your head. Hold it in …two …three …
   - Breathe Out: Exhale to the bottoms of your feet. Release. Give it all up to the squeegee. Hold it out …two …three …
   - Smile: Resume your normal breathing pattern. Smile. Say "ahh."

3. Use a Super Habit trigger to remind you to practice your Squeegee Breath during your practice day.

Squeegee Breath ACTION STEPS

- What is your squeegee trigger?
- How will you track the number of Squeegee Breaths you take a day?
- How will you celebrate each breath?
- What is your reward for your first "10-Squeegee Day"?
- Who is the first person you want to teach the Squeegee Breath to?
- Journal on your experience.

THE BID TEAM HUDDLE

The Squeegee Breath is about who you are being. It does not change the structure of your day. The next several tools, starting here with the BID Team Huddle, will change the structure and stresses of your practice day. This allows you to combine changes in who you are being with a change in what you are doing for an additional drop in the stresses of your practice.

Team Huddle Power Training

A well-done BID Huddle with your practice team is the single most powerful stress reduction technique for physicians after regular use of the Squeegee Breath. It amazes me how many doctors skip a team huddle because they are too busy. I believe the reason is because it is very easy to do a team huddle poorly. Let me show you what I call *Team Huddle Power Training* so you can learn the how to use a three-minute huddle to save you forty-five minutes a day.

You are most likely familiar with the concept of a team huddle. You may have even tried it and seen it be only temporarily effective. The most common reason for a huddle having only a temporary effect is the doctor stops calling the huddle. What a tragic missed opportunity, though I understand why it happens. Survival mode and a team huddle are incompatible with each other.

It is easy to feel like you are too busy to do anything but dive right into the chaos of your day and start seeing patients. "We don't have time to huddle; there are patients in rooms." This is a missed opportunity to be proactive about your patient flow and get home sooner.

Your team huddle is an investment in a smooth practice day. Every minute in a well-run huddle will save you a minimum of five later on and dramatically lower the stress level for you and your team members by putting out fires before they start.

Why BID

Most physicians have a half-day schedule. You have a block of patients you see in the morning and another block in the afternoon. It is natural to huddle up and preview your half-day schedule in the morning and again after lunch in most practices. If your practice is not structured exactly like this, do not abandon the huddle—instead, modify your huddle(s) so they work for you and your team.

<u>**Example:**</u>

If you do cases in the OR in the morning and see patients in the office in the afternoon, you have two work teams. Huddle with the OR team in the morning and your office team before you start your afternoon office hours. Make sense?

<u>**The basic team huddle process**</u>

- Make time for the huddle—just three minutes before each half-day. However, you must block it out and arrange for your team to meet before you start patient hours. Remember, this is an investment in everyone's peace of mind.
- Grab your schedule for the half-day coming up—paper or electronic.
- Huddle up with all the members of your patient flow team. Reception, nurse or other roomer, MAs, PAs, NPs …anyone who is part of the team moving your patients through the flow of your practice.
- Run through the schedule.
  - ‣ Which patient has special needs or should be in a special room?
  - ‣ Which one is upset, angry, or really sick?
  - ‣ Do you have the test results and reports you need for today's visit? If not, who is going to run them down? (NOTE: It is best to run this lab and report check the day before or earlier in a separate visit prep process. This is just a final check in the huddle.)
  - ‣ What open slots do you have in the schedule, and what do you want the team to do with them?
- Add anything any member of the team wants to share with or request from the other team members that would help patient flow go more smoothly.

That is as far as most people take the process of a team huddle. It can be so much more. Here are the power-training points I encourage you to incorporate in your huddles.

<u>**Team huddle power points**</u>

1. You go to them.

Do not make the team come to your office where you sit behind your desk.

What message does that send? You are the king or queen and they are peons. Think about this for a moment. In the half hour before you see your first patient, what is the rest of your team doing? They are busy. They are setting you up to hit the ground running with scheduled patient number one.

I strongly suggest you go to their location. What message does that send? We are all in this together. We are a team and I am *not* the king or queen. This approach is much more collaborative, team-centered, and ultimately, much more effective.

2. Make a human connection.

Make sure you check in with your team. Ask how everyone is doing. Make sure you know whose birthday it is, who is pregnant, who is doing well, and who is stressed today. The huddle is an important opportunity for a quick person-to-person check in. Don't miss it.

3. Squeegee in and out.

I strongly recommend you start and end the huddle with a Squeegee Breath. You might say something like, "Hey everyone, let's take a big breath and get really present here in the huddle." (In to the top…two…three…Out to the feet…two…three. Ahh.)

Complete the huddle.

"Hey everyone, let's do one more of those big breaths and let it all go before we head out."

Remember, you are a certified Squeegee Breath trainer. It can be that simple, and I guarantee everyone will appreciate it.

4. Delegate responsibility for the huddle.

The reason the BID Huddle is not universal is simple: doctors usually call them, and we are simply not reliable. We get too busy. Our Lone Ranger programming has us believing we have to be the one in charge. So, when we stop calling the team together after a couple days, another huddle dies a quiet death.

The solution is to delegate the calling of the huddle to someone other than the doctor on the team. Make it their responsibility. This eliminates your need to depend on willpower or memory to get it done. You can even delegate the steps in the huddle to your designated Huddle Champion. If you decide to do this, remember to give them permission to force you to attend when you try skip out of the huddle down the road—because you know you will, sooner or later.

It could sound like this:

>*Elizabeth, I would like you to call the team together in our BID Huddles and run the process. Let's see how that goes, because I don't trust myself to be as consistent as I know you are.*
>
>*I would like us to huddle before each half-day every time, because we both know it makes a difference. Also, I want to give you permission to call me on it if I try to skip the huddle. I know there will come a time when I will try to let it slide. I am telling you now, you have my permission to remind me that you are in charge of the huddle, and the goal is BID every day, and that includes me.*
>
>*How does that sound and feel to you?*

5. Have some fun.

The huddle is a great place to sing happy birthday, give high fives, and even put your hands in the middle and make a noise at the end. You can do things like go around the circle and everyone says one word that sums up how they are feeling today. The sky's the limit on fun and creativity in your huddles.

BID Huddle ACTION STEPS

- Who is on your BID Huddle Team?
- When does it make sense to hold your huddles? (You can ask the team this question, too. Let go of your Lone Ranger. When you find yourself struggling to answer a question, let them help you.)
- When will you tell your team and get started?
- What is one fun thing you would like to do in your huddles?
- Who could you delegate the BID Huddle to?
- When will you do that?
- Journal on your experience.

BATCH PROCESSING

DOCTORS ARE A lot like dogs in some ways. If a dog is sitting on the porch and I get its attention and throw a tennis ball, it can't *not* chase it. It can't resist.

With doctors, the tennis ball is a refill request that pops up on your EMR screen. It is not urgent, but how often do you drop what you are doing to address it?

We mistake *every* action as an *urgent* one and chase them just like the dog and the tennis ball.

Add in test results, phone messages, and referral paperwork, and your day is fractured into a hundred pieces for one simple reason: you are taking care of these items one at a time and allowing them to interrupt your patient flow.

Sure, they only take two to three minutes each. Add it up, though, and you will get sixty to ninety minutes of wasted time in your day. No other industry would allow that kind of inefficiency. Yet in medicine, it is every doctor for himself when it comes to figuring out how to handle these non-urgent tasks. No one teaches you how to do a good job.

The solution is batch processing

Tasks that are non-urgent can be batched and done all at once, in a batch, twice a day. In the days of paper charts, we used to put out a basket for each task type. Refills go in this basket. Test results go in that one when they return.

Twice a day you "run the basket" and boom, boom, boom …all of the tasks are done.

In a standard office day where you have an a.m. and a p.m. schedule, some good times to do batch processing are 11:30 a.m. and 4:30 p.m. That way the morning's work is done before lunch and the afternoon's work is done before you go home.

EMR makes this a little different. Often, these non-urgent tasks pop up as alerts on your tablet, laptop, or desktop screen. These prompts are equally enticing to our dog-like "fetch" mechanism and even more powerful time wasters.

Batch these, too, by *not* addressing them when they come in. Make a "virtual basket" that you run in a batch twice a day.

What can you batch in your practice?

Tip #1: Use Your Team

Ask your team this same question, and let them join in the effort to get you out of the office by six.

"What tasks happen every day—things that are not urgent, yet have to be done before the day is over? Where we can put them in batches and do them all at once, twice a day?"

"Which ones require my MD-level attention, and which can be done by someone else on the team?"

Tip #2: Hide the Batches

One way to mess up batch processing is batch peeking. This is when you have a system to make batches of the tasks as they come in—and you break the new rules by looking at the batch and doing the tasks when it is not one of your two designated times in the day.

Example:

You put a basket at the nurses' station to hold the returning test reports. Your plan is to process what is in the basket twice a day. However, you find yourself constantly looking in the basket as you walk by and processing the one or two items you find there. You might say "batch processing doesn't work for me." We both know that is not true.

The solution to this is simple. You cannot be trusted to play by the new rules here. Have your nurse or assistant *hide the basket*. They only bring it out when it is time to run the batch. This works well when your batch is physical reports, and you are putting them in a physical basket.

Batching of digital tasks has its own challenges. The key here is to set up a system that does not allow you to easily sabotage the batching process.

Example: Old-School Solution to a Digital Time Waster

I have a client who was extremely distracted by the instant messenger function on her EMR. All of the staff would relay IMs for each patient phone message and refill. They would pop up on her tablet computer as a little flashing counter—like the old "You've got mail" function back in the day.

Her IT people said there was no way to disable the counter from appearing on the face of her tablet, so we went old-school.

Now, she uses a little Post-it note. She puts in on the tablet screen over the counter so she can't see the messages as they come in. That small portion of the screen is covered by the Post-It® note. She takes it off at 11:30 a.m. and 4:30 p.m. to run the batch of messages.

Batching is a test of your creativity.

You can batch anything. Sometimes, you must build a system that takes the doctor completely out of the picture. Sometimes, you have to go old-school. The key here is not giving up and making sure you don't Lone Ranger this. If you find yourself sitting alone in your office trying to figure this out and coming up empty, you have an opportunity to rise above your programming.

Remember to ask your team for help.

You are never alone in the office. It is not your job to figure this out all on your own. Use your team. I know they want to help.

- Ask them for suggestions on creating the system.
- Ask them to help you implement it.
- Ask them to help design a simple way to track how batch processing is going.
- Thank them for their help and support. Treat them like dogs for sure.

Batch processing ACTION STEPS

- What is the first task you would like to batch?
- How would you and your team like to create the batch? (Don't forget to ask your team here!)
- What is the first step?
- When will you take that step?
- How will you track your performance?
- When will you revisit the system?
- Journal on your experience.

BROKEN RECORD AUTOMATION

Do you ever feel like a broken record in the office?

You know the old vinyl albums we played back in the day on a phonograph with a needle? Sometimes, they would skip and play the same thing over and over until you grabbed the needle and picked it up from the face of the spinning black disc. Do you ever feel like that during your week in the office?

Do you find yourself saying the same thing over and over again to your patients?

Do you ever find yourself typing the same thing over and over into the EMR?

Every time you get stuck in this cycle, your patient flow comes to a complete halt. The whole office is waiting on you to move on, and you are stuck …just like the needle on that old vinyl record.

Not only that, this "broken record" repetition can be a major source of stress, because what you are doing doesn't even require the skills and experience of a physician. An automatically generated chart note or recorded instructional video could completely and adequately take your place in these broken record moments. You did not go to medical school for this.

Rather than clench your jaw and growl the next time you feel like a broken record, let me encourage you to do something else instead.

Smile. Here's why …

This broken record is a red flag that marks the quickest ways to improve your patient flow and optimize your office day. When you deal with broken record behaviors properly, you will automatically improve patient flow, dramatically lower your stress levels, and get home sooner every day you are in the office.

Broken record = automate & delegate

You transform the broken record into better patient flow by automating and/or delegating the repeated activity. In my work with overstressed doctors, we have found the broken record occurs most predictably in the patient education and documentation phases of your practice activities.

If you are typing the same thing into your EMR time and time again, this is a screaming opportunity to create a template. With a template, the broken record turns into a simple keystroke or click of the mouse to enter the template in a single *schwack*. See more of a suggested EMR strategy earlier in this chapter.

Let's look closer at patient education broken record opportunities.

Even though every specialty is different, you have a small number of diagnoses that make up a significant portion of your practice. The 80-20 rule is a universal law of nature. It applies in your practice, too. Twenty percent of your diagnoses account for 80 percent of the time and energy you devote to patient education.

You will find yourself interrupting your patient flow to educate the patient on this relatively small set of diagnoses—over and over and over again. It is a classic broken record and an opportunity to slice minutes off of your office day with automation and delegation.

Three broken record solutions for patient education

1. Handout System

Make a handout with the broken record information on it. Put some of your personality and your specific tips and tools in there. Print it on colored paper so your instructions stand out from the sheaf of other white papers your patients take home from every office visit, most of which have to do with insurance or billing.

Keep all of your patient education handouts in an accordion file in the exam room, so it is a snap for you to find the one you want and hand it to your patient at the end of the visit.

2. Delegate to Your Team

Delegate patient education to a staff member. Train them on what to say and how to say it—perhaps with a handout as above. Once you have seen the patient, made the diagnosis, and patient education is clearly the next step, call your patient educator into the exam room to deliver the handout and the verbal teaching. You can kick patient flow back into gear by moving on to the next room.

3. Video System

Shoot a video of you delivering a primetime version of your patient education. Load your patient education videos onto an iPad, laptop, or your own YouTube channel. When patient education is the next step in the patient flow, hand the patient the video player and start the video. Tell your nurse the patient is watching the video and to check in with the patient in a couple minutes while you move on to the next room. You will also want a take-home handout to go with these videos.

If you are comfortable making your videos public, you can also give the patient a handout with a link to the video on YouTube, so they can watch from their computer at home.

One at a time

The plate spinning theory holds here as well. Don't let yourself get overwhelmed creating a huge library of patient education materials all at once. Just like the plate spinner, the best way is to take this project on one diagnosis at a time. **Each time you automate patient education for another diagnosis, your day just got shorter.**

If you put some personality and solid information into your materials, they will do a better job of education than you talking off the cuff on a busy day for the sixth time about the same issue.

Broken Record ACTION STEPS

- What are the diagnoses where you most frequently feel like a broken record?
- What technology would you like to use to teach your patients?
- Which diagnosis would you like to take on first?
- What is the first step to get started?
- Who on your team can help? (Don't forget to ask your team!)
- Journal on your experience.

QUADRANT II: PERSONAL RECHARGE

"There's no such thing as work-life balance. There are work-life choices, and you make them, and they have consequences."
—Jack Welch

"Happiness is not a matter of intensity but of balance, order, rhythm, and harmony."
—Thomas Merton

NOW, WE SHIFT focus from relieving stress to enabling more effective recharge when you are off work. Most of these tools are focused on creating more life balance. Before I show you how to create work balance between your practice and your larger life, I can't help but be distracted by yet another flashing red light and screaming siren trying to get our attention dead ahead. Are you noticing it, too? Wait a minute, the red light is spelling something out now. It says …

DILEMMA ALERT …DILEMMA ALERT . . .

That's right—work-life balance is not a problem, either.

There is no simple, one-step solution to work-life balance. This is not because it is impossible to solve, but because work-life balance is not a problem.

Work-life balance is another dilemma.

Let's stop looking for a solution, rise up and out of victim mode, and get going on the tasks to address a dilemma.

1. **DEFINE** the two horns of the dilemma and the optimum balance point.
2. Design a **STRATEGY** to create the balance you seek.
3. Build a **SYSTEM** to monitor the effectiveness of your strategy.
4. **TWEAK** your strategy and your system as often as needed.

Work-life balance is something you must attend to regularly using a multi-part strategy. If you are not paying attention to it at least twice a month, you will be out of balance shortly.

The two horns of the dilemma are clearly visible this time. Our job is to turn what is usually a battle into a balancing act of …

Work vs. Life

The balance point you seek is the time and energy devoted to each. You feel you are doing a good job and making enough money at work *and* your life outside of work is fulfilling and well-rounded.

The reason work and life seem to be in direct conflict so often is simple. The time and energy required for each comes out of the same pie. Each must take from the other, because the pie is finite. Here is what the conflict can often feel like.

Remember the 800-pound gorilla?

Imagine that you share your house, your personal living space, with an 800-pound, silverback lowland gorilla. When you come home, he is at the door. He has been in the house alone all day. As you squeeze through the front door, imagine how much of your house would you have to yourself. This is a wild gorilla, mind you.

You would be relegated to the corners of the room. The gorilla would give you the scraps of space at the edges, take everything else for himself, and make a mess of everything in sight.

What happens to your house when you live with a gorilla is a lot like what happens to your life when you choose medicine as a career. Your life outside of medicine gets crowded out. You are left with scraps along the edges for all your free time and important relationships. The career that was supposed to enable an extraordinary life now dominates your life, leaving little room for anything else.

Gorilla Taming

All is not lost. Gorillas can be house-trained, tamed, and shown healthy boundaries. You can do the same with your medical career when you know how. It will take a strategy to manage this balancing act. The following tools from Quadrant II of the Matrix are a good place to begin.

THE SCHEDULE HACK

ONE OF THE laws of your work-life balance strategy is "the strongest structure wins." When we are talking about your schedule, the structure required is a calendar. Let me ask you a quick question:

Do you carry a calendar at work?

I know your answer is yes.

If I asked you to hand me your calendar, what would I find on it? It would have your work and call schedule for sure. After all, it is the calendar you carry to work.

What else is on this calendar?

Would I find any of the following?

- Your spouse or significant other's schedule?
- Your children's schedule?
- Your workout schedule?
- Your next date night?
- Your next vacation?
- Some blocked off free time for yourself to be with friends, take a walk, hike, bike ride, yoga or cooking class, or read a book for pleasure (heavens, just imagine that for a moment will you)?

If you have all of those on the calendar you carry at work, congratulations. Take a moment to pat yourself on the back, because I have never seen it happen—and I have asked thousands of doctors what is on their calendars.

Understand this as an actual law of life balance.

Anything not on the calendar you are carrying is _not_ going to happen, period.

One of the keys to taming the gorilla is to always carry something more than your work schedule with you. If you want to have time for your life, you must carry your Life Calendar with you at all times as well. Let me say that again.

If you want to have a life, _always_ carry your Life Calendar with you.

The Schedule Hack is a process a coaching client and I invented so you always have your Life Calendar in your pocket or purse—without having to purchase or learn any new technology. This is the first step in showing that gorilla some healthy boundaries.

The Schedule Hack has an added bonus as well. It will also bring you closer with your friends and family when they see you making them a priority every week.

Schedule Hack materials

1. The paper calendar you have hanging at home on the side of the fridge. It's the one with kitties or landscapes or your favorite poems you bought at Christmas. This calendar usually contains only the children's schedule or nothing at all. NOTE: If you prefer to use an electronic calendar such as Google Calendar and are skilled with it, go for it. This version of the Schedule Hack is meant to be old-school so anyone can implement it today. If you and your family are facile with multiple Google Calendars at once, be my guest as long as it actually works to create the work-life balance you seek. If it does not, I highly recommend this calendar-on-the-fridge method.
2. Some colored pens—your favorite kind.
3. Your cell phone.

SCHEDULE HACK PROCEDURE

Step One: Build Your Life Calendar for the Week Ahead

Pick a time in the week where everyone in your family or household is available. It could be just you or it could be you, your spouse or significant other, all your kids, and your parents who live over the garage. Whatever "family" is to you, pick a time when all of you can get together for a half hour or so. Sunday in late mornings often works well.

Pull that paper calendar off the fridge, grab the pens, and put them all on the kitchen table. Have everyone grab their calendars for the week ahead and put them on the table, too.

Have some fun, be creative, and build your family calendar for the week ahead. Put everyone's schedule on it, using the colors however they make sense.

Remember your schedule, too.

I know you will put your work schedule and call days on here automatically. That is on autopilot. This is a chance to schedule in the activities of your life outside of medicine. This is where you build your strategy to create more balance between your work and your larger life. This is where gorilla training begins.

What do you want *for yourself* in the upcoming week? Remember, if you don't put it on your Life Calendar right here and now, it will not happen in the week ahead.

- Workouts
- Free time
- Coffee with an old friend or a relative
- Time to read a book
- A class or hike
- A date night

Whatever you want, you must put it down on the calendar. Do it now (see the Weekly Bucket List training later in this section for more ideas).

Mandatory Final Scheduling Action:

The last thing you put on the calendar is the date and time of your next Schedule Hack session. Everyone needs to be clear on when you will meet again. If I meet you in the street and ask you to show me your Life Calendar, it must have your next Schedule Hack session on it—agreed?

Step Two: Take a Picture of Your Life Calendar with Your Cell Phone

Yes, it really can be that easy. Your Life Calendar can now be in your pocket at all times right there on your cell phone.

Step Three: Defend Your Life Calendar

Now you are prepared to say the two-letter magic word of work-life balance. *No.*

If someone at work asks you to take an extra call day or work a few extra hours, you can say, "Hang on a second, and let me check my calendar."

Open up your cell phone to the picture of your Life Calendar and see if you have a scheduled activity. If you are already booked, you can say, "I'm sorry, I have another commitment at that time. I won't be able to help out."

As you read the conversation above, does it make you a little uncomfortable? Most doctors squirm when I demonstrate this bit of dialogue. We are horrible at saying *no*. Our discomfort has several sources.

- We are completely out of practice at saying *no*. That is okay. Saying *no* is a skill you can practice. Remember, "Practice Makes _____."

- You don't want to be perceived as not being a team player. This is a variation on the prime directive of *never show weakness.*
- Let's face it—you won't always say *no,* even if you have a conflict on your Life Calendar.

Here is how to address these concerns.

a. Practice

Stand in front of a mirror and practice several different ways to say *no* until you find a turn of phrase you are at least moderately comfortable with. Here are some examples:

- *I'm sorry, I have a previous engagement.*
- *Nope, I'm booked at that time.*
- *Looks like that time is taken, sorry.*
- *Not happening; looks like it's my date night* (if that is true).

The possibilities are endless. The key is to be prepared, practiced, and polished when the opportunity arises.

> ## Power Tip:
> **Role-play with your spouse or significant other. Have them be one of your partners—perhaps the one most likely to ask you to cover for them. You be yourself saying, "No."**
> **Rehearse until your spouse or significant other gives you at least a B+ for your performance. Have some fun here.**

b. Release the Head Trash of "Always"

You will not always say *no* to this request when it comes at you. You can let "always" go. Let's shoot for 85 percent of the time, instead. The main reasons you won't say *no* are as follows:

- You owe this person. They covered for you at an earlier date and you want to settle the debt.
- You want this person to owe you down the road, so you can call on that debt in the future.
- You are not confident enough in your ability to say *no* yet to give it a shot. Time for more practice.

When you carry your Life Calendar, see a conflict, and say *yes* anyway, you will see immediately which member of your family deserves an apology.

The Schedule Hack allows you to live your life in alignment with your complete circle of priorities.

I can assure you it works every time you use it. The key is to put it into action now that you understand the principles involved.

Here is a common scenario. You certainly carry your work calendar at all times; I know that about you. If you are a parent, your kids' schedules are in that calendar too. Most likely, the only thing missing is you. If that is the case, a Schedule Hack upgrade is what you are looking for.

Keep doing your weekly calendar coordination with your family; just add you into the picture. Put your exercise schedule in there, your date nights, or some unscheduled down time.

Power Tip:
Scheduled Spontaneity

This is a very useful concept and a little-understood work-life balance power tool. Scheduled Spontaneity is when you block off a chunk of time on your calendar and defend that time like you would any other Life Calendar event, without scheduling a specific activity in that slot.

The time is free and protected. When you get to this time block, you can be completely spontaneous about what you do in the moment. One excellent use of Scheduled Spontaneity is one-on-one alone time with your children. You block out the time and let your child choose what the two of you will do when you are together. They love that, and there is no pressure on you to figure things out ahead of time.

Give it a try, and see how it works for you.

It is one of the options available for your Schedule Hack.

Schedule Hack ACTION STEPS

- Who are the people on your Life Calendar?
- When is a good time for you all to do the Schedule Hack together?
- If you need to buy a paper calendar or pens, when will you do that?
- When will you do your first Schedule Hack? How can you make it fun?
- What things will you put on the calendar just for you?
- When will you practice saying *no*? (I dare you to practice with your spouse or significant other and find a way to make it fun!)
- Journal on your experience.

DATE NIGHT SECRETS

A STANDING ITEM on your Life Calendar *must* be at least two date nights a month with your spouse or significant other.

Do not skip date night. Don't let it slide or forget to schedule it—even if you are single.

A date night every week is even better, as long as you understand some of the basic rules of date nights.

NOTE: If you do not have a significant other, date night could be an actual date with another person, time with a friend, or doing something nice or unexpected all by yourself. Yes, indeed, you can take yourself out on date night, too.

Fun and adventure

When you are really busy, figuring out what to do on your date night can seem like just another item on your task list. I encourage you to do an attitude check here. What is more important to you—the 800-pound gorilla or some love, romance, adventure, and fun? Date night is a chance to break out of survival mode and do something extraordinary.

A Few Ideas

- Take turns deciding what you will do on date night. The one who is planning the date can't tell the other where you are going or what you are doing (other than what to wear).
- Each of you put three date night ideas on slips of paper and drop them into a hat. Pick one, raffle style, and go for it.
- Make it a game and set rules. Here is a fun one: Your date night can't involve calories or money.

Mandatory Final Date Night Action:

Schedule the next date night as the last action of this date night. If I meet you in the street and ask you to show me your Life Calendar, it must have your next date night on it, agreed?

Power Tip:

I encourage you to go the extra yard for date night. My challenge to you is to schedule a minimum of two date nights on your Life Calendar each month for the next three months—if your call schedule allows you to look that far into the future. Just walk over to the calendar on the fridge and write them in now. Then, at the end of this week's date night, write in another for three months from now, knowing there is a minimum of six more between now and then. There's some work-life balance for you.

Date Night ACTION STEPS

- When is your next date night?
- Who is doing the planning?
- Discuss scheduling date nights out three months.
- Then, do it.
- Remember, your date night is not over until you have scheduled the next one and put it on both of your life calendars.
- Journal on your experience.

BUCKET LIST SECRETS

BUCKET LIST (NOUN): The list of things you want to do before you "kick the bucket."

My clients and I find it very useful to build two bucket lists and use them as additional work-life balance tools.

1. Your BIG Bucket List

These are the classic *things I must do before I die*. The challenge with creating a meaningful BIG Bucket List is that most people put way too many things on it. This sets you up to use the BIG Bucket List to beat yourself up. If you put too many items on there, you will notice you are never crossing any of them off and feel guilty.

A real BIG Bucket List is not simply a list of things you want to check off before your time is up. An authentic BIG Bucket List contains the life-altering, mind-bending

---

Power Tip:
Your BIG Bucket List "acid test"

My daughter, Rose, has expressed an interest to go to Africa ever since she was a little girl. She even went so far as to schedule a trip once, with money down, but she had to cancel at the last minute. In my effort to understand whether Africa was actually on her BIG Bucket List, I asked her a question.

"Rose, imagine many years in the future and you are an old woman. You are in the hospital because you are sick. You are sick enough that you and the doctors both know you will never make it out of the hospital. You will die here. Imagine I came to visit you and sat down by the edge of your bed and asked if you ever got a chance to take that trip to Africa. Imagine you had to say no because you never made the trip. How would that feel?"

Rose was twenty at the time, but when I asked her that question, she answered in the voice of a six-year-old girl. "Oh Daddy, I would die right there."

That is one of Rose's BIG Bucket List items.

things, the ones that would break your heart if you were *not* able to accomplish them in this lifetime.

This question is taken from the book *The Five Wishes* by Gay Hendricks. It is the best way I know to radically shorten your BIG Bucket List and use it to start living your most closely-held dreams.

No one gets out of here alive. Now is the time to build that list and get on it, especially if the last couple of years or decades have been devoted to your career rather than your larger life. There is some rebalancing to be had.

BIG Bucket List ACTION STEPS

Make your BIG Bucket List. Write it down. Keep it in the folder with your Ideal Practice Description and Master Plan.

Put the items on your BIG Bucket List to the question I asked my daughter Rose above. Give someone else the list and have him or her read that scenario for each item. Circle the ones that pass the test—the ones that would break your heart if you did not accomplish them.

BIG Bucket List Check Off

Now, it is time to get one of these BIG bucket list items on your Life Calendar. Normally, these are pretty big-ticket items. The key is to look out on your calendar as far as you need to look. In some cases, it could even be next year. Look out until you can see the space you require to do this thing well, and block it off.

Then, pay for the tickets.

If there is one thing that will get a doctor to actually take a trip, it is having money down. So, block off the time and buy the tickets now. Whether it is Machu Picchu, Africa like my Rosie, the running of the bulls in Pamplona, visiting the country of your family's origin, a Spanish immersion school in Costa Rica, rafting the Grand Canyon …get it scheduled and paid for, and it is highly likely to actually take place.

Afterward, it will take its rightful place in your memories as a peak experience, rather than a heartbreaking regret.

2. Your Weekly Bucket List

Is there something you have found that is guaranteed to make your week special? Is there an activity or experience that turns your whole week around every time you do it and you say, "Man, I wish I could do that every week. It would make a huge difference for me."

Typically, these are activities you only manage to squeeze in every once in a while. I think you know what I am talking about. What is that activity that makes all the difference for you? This very short list is something I call your Weekly Bucket List. These are the things you want to put in every week come rain or shine.

Here are some examples I have heard from physician clients:

- Cycling
- Running
- Yoga
- Hiking
- Coffee with a friend or colleague
- Alone time with each of your children—one-on-one
- Family play time as a whole family
- Reading a book for pleasure
- Meditation
- Mani-pedi
- Massage
- Date night (Yes, things can show up on multiple lists. It just shows how important they are.)
- Scheduled Spontaneity (see above)

Make sure you bring your Weekly Bucket List items to your Schedule Hack each week. Putting these items on your Life Calendar is part of carving out time and space for you in your busy week. Defend these items just as vigorously as you do your work schedule to show that gorilla some healthy boundaries.

Guilt Can Come Up Here

Some people have problems with guilt as they contemplate this concept of doing something just for themselves. A little voice saying, *What makes you think you are so special?* can pop up when you are blocking off time for your own personal use. This is your programming, pure and simple.

You can tell that voice, *thank you for sharing* and do it anyhow. It is only when you are able to experience the pleasant things in your life that you can understand the difference that can make for you, your patients, your team, and your family.

Remember, plate spinning applies here as well. If yoga makes a night and day difference in your week, for example...

- Schedule one yoga class in the week ahead.
- Defend the schedule.
- Do it.
- See how it feels and whether you want to make yoga a Weekly Bucket List item in your Life Calendar going forward.

Weekly Bucket List ACTION STEPS

- What's on your Weekly Bucket List?
- When can you schedule it?
- How can you make it an every week, or every other week, standing item?
- Journal on your experience.

THE BOUNDARY RITUAL

ONE OF THE keys to being able to recharge when you are not at work is creating a clean, solid, functioning boundary between work and home.

Leave work at work and come all the way home

This boundary exists so you leave work at work, rather than dragging the stress and busyness of it home with you. Without a clean boundary, your energy and awareness remains at least partially focused on your practice, even when you are not in the office or hospital.

Rather than finding an oasis of rejuvenation at home, the drain of work stress continues.

Creating a Boundary Ritual is a skill you can learn and practice. It is the energetic equivalent of punching the time clock and checking out of your role as doctor. Your Boundary Ritual marks the boundary between work and home.

Your Boundary Ritual marks the transition from the environment where the patient comes first to one where _you_ come first.

Fortunately, we have an excellent role model of a Boundary Ritual—Mr. Rogers.

Yes, _that_ Mr. Rogers from _Mister Rogers' Neighborhood_, the children's television show on PBS.

You don't know what Mr. Rogers does before he walks through that door. It only takes a couple of shows to realize he is not the real Mr. Rogers until he has done three things. Remember them?

1. Put on his zip-up cardigan
2. Change his shoes
3. Sing his song, _It's a beautiful day in the neighborhood, a beautiful day for a neighbor— would you be mine . . ._

With his Boundary Ritual complete, he is the Mr. Rogers we know and love for the rest of the show.

I have heard of physicians who naturally understand the importance of a Boundary Ritual. One friend's father—a small town family doc—would shower and change clothes after coming home every day. He wouldn't talk to his family until this Boundary Ritual was complete.

I strongly encourage you to develop your own Boundary Ritual. It can be any action you wish, as long as your intention is to let go of being a doctor and come all the way home.

You have an excellent tool already available in the Squeegee Breath.

You also have a whole new set of Super Habit triggers within whatever routine it takes for you to get from your practice to your home.

The simplest Boundary Ritual is to use a Squeegee Breath to release your role as doctor, using something you always do on your way home as your trigger. It could be closing your office door on the way out, taking the key out of your car's ignition at home, opening the door of your house, and many more.

Other examples include:
- Taking a shower
- Changing your clothes
- Taking out your contacts
- Going for a walk, run, or bike ride
- Walking the dog

What you use for a Boundary Ritual is not as important as having one in the first place. Set your intention to come all the way home. Feel the release of your doctor responsibilities as you perform your ritual and let the recharge soak in.

Don't be afraid to experiment here. Try different rituals out to see how they work. Remember Practice Makes [_____] applies to your Boundary Ritual skills, too. Switch things up, and develop a small handful of your favorites. Smile, breathe, and release the doctor completely until the next time you need to put on your white coat.

NOTE: There will be times when you are at home and still working, like when you are on call or have charting you intend to do from home. Save the Boundary Ritual for when your work is done—then, do the deed and form the boundary.

Power Tip:

A commute is an excellent place to build your Boundary Ritual. Pick some soothing music, put some items you find comforting on the dash of your car, take some deep breaths, and use the ride home as a decompression and extended release of your role as a physician.

You can pack dozens of Squeegee Breaths into your drive and hit the front door with the doctor completely turned off.

Boundary Ritual ACTION STEPS

- What is your Boundary Ritual?
- When will you start using it?
- Journal on your experience.

QUADRANT III: ORGANIZATIONAL STRESS RELIEF

"Management is doing things right; leadership is doing the right things."
—Peter Drucker

*"God grant me the serenity to accept the things I cannot change,
the courage to change the things I can,
and the wisdom to know the difference."*
—The Serenity Prayer

QUADRANT III IS where you and your organization can work together to help lower your stress and prevent burnout. You can focus your cooperative efforts on creating a more physician-friendly workplace—by design and on purpose.

Over the last three years, I have constructed and tested what I believe to be the shortest path to meaningful change in the workplace environment and group culture of any healthcare organization. This was developed in response to a statement I hear often from healthcare leaders. It goes something like this: "We would like to do something about the physicians' stress levels, but where do you even get started?"

This is typically said with a shrug of the shoulders and a prayer that I will drop the subject. It is as if lowering stress in the frontlines of healthcare is some unsolvable mystery, dark, brooding, and unapproachable. Balderdash.

The tools to create a more physician-friendly work environment are simple common sense, just like everything you have learned so far. It only takes three steps to produce rapid, significant change inside an organization. I call these steps the Physician Engagement Formula.

THE PHYSICIAN ENGAGEMENT FORMULA

1. Fill the educational hole around burnout.
2. Survey the providers for their specific practice stressors.
3. Address those concerns with a physician-led Burnout Prevention Working Group.

When done well, these three steps will not only create a more physician-friendly workplace, but they will also instill a culture of support, respect, and trust where one may have never existed before.

Let's take these steps one at a time.

1. Fill the educational hole around burnout for physicians and frontline staff

All burnout prevention efforts must start with education. I have already shown you how much of burnout's power lies in its ability to hide in our blind spots and programming. I have also shared a number of tools in Quadrants I and II that should be part of the normal education process of any doctor or nurse.

Unfortunately, we both know these concepts are not taught in medical school or residency. In fact, the first time most physicians learn about burnout is when they are already in its downward spiral.

If you want to equip your physicians and staff with the tools to prevent burnout, the organization will have to take responsibility. You have taken responsibility for your own education by reading this book for personal benefit. Your organization can provide a training hub for all the providers and staff it employs.

You can pick a date to "out" burnout.

A comprehensive approach to this education process can even allow you to pick a date when everyone in your organization can recognize burnout and has Quadrant I and II tools to deal effectively with stress in the workplace.

I recommend a three-pronged approach:

- Live burnout prevention training such as our *Burnout Proof* workshop.
- Video burnout prevention training for those who cannot make the live event. Our *Burnout Prevention Video Training Series* is an example.
- Incorporate burnout prevention training into your onboarding process to maintain 100 percent awareness of burnout in the workplace.

Universal burnout education produces some interesting cultural changes.

- It is no longer taboo to talk about stress, burnout, and work-life balance.
- It is no longer taboo to admit you are overstressed and reach out for help and support.
- Colleagues will begin to ask each other if they are okay, rising above the Lone Ranger, superhero, and *never show weakness* programming.

- Stress levels in the providers and staff begin to have a place in the leadership conversations throughout your organization.
- It sends a powerful message that the organization cares about its people—if steps two and three below follow in short order.

2. Survey the providers about their top three daily stresses

It is amazing to me how rarely organizations ask their physicians to name the top stresses in their workdays. If an organization does survey the doctors, it is usually with a huge, expensive third party survey that does not ask questions that generate actionable results.

Ideally, you are surveying your providers with a short, focused, inexpensive question set at regular intervals and acting on the information they provide.

Here is my recommended question set:

- How would you rate your satisfaction with your career in our organization on a 1-10 scale?
- What are the top three stresses in your workday?
- How would you describe the culture around here?
- What would you like the culture to be?

I send these surveys out using Google Drive. They are fast and free. You will have your answers back in less than a week. Notice that your question about the top three stressors will give you immediately actionable data.

The doctors tell you what is frying their bacon. They are pointing where they want the organization to pitch in. All you have to do is let them know you heard them and get on their concerns with meaningful action. That leads us to step three.

3. Create a Physician Burnout Working Group to address the physicians' concerns

The best way for an organization to show it cares about the health of the providers in the front lines is to create, support, and fund a Burnout Prevention Working Group.

Note that this is not a committee. Committees have meetings. Most meetings in healthcare organizations are of stunningly poor quality. A working group does work. The entire focus of this working group is to make progress in creating a more physician-friendly workplace.

The project list for this group comes directly from the surveys outlined above. You asked the doctors a direct question. They have given you a direct answer. Now, it is time to take meaningful action.

It is critical that the working group receives funding and administrative support.

I see lots of burnout prevention committees with no staff and no budget. This guarantees it will fail to generate a meaningful and lasting response to the doctors' concerns. The meetings will dissolve into ineffective hand wringing.

Ideally, the Burnout Prevention Working Group is an arm of your existing physician leadership structure. It must have physicians as its major participants. When this is true, the committee serves a dual purpose:

1. It is a proactive force for positive change in the organization.
2. The members of the group are able to hone their leadership and project management skills as they address the challenges identified by the survey. It is a training ground for your physician leaders where they can practice leading successful projects. They are then able to bring their improved skills back into all facets of your physician leadership activities.

The Results

The three steps in the Physician Engagement Formula—when they are done well—combine to continue producing positive changes in your group culture.

Your providers will begin to notice and respond:

- "You taught me about burnout—how to recognize and prevent it."
- "You ask me what I would like changed around here and listen to what I have to say."
- "You are actually working to make my life better here at work."

These three steps build trust between the organization and the frontline providers. They start to shift from the Lone Ranger culture to one of mutual support and caring.

Unfortunately, less than 10 percent of organizations do anything like this, in my experience. It is a tremendous missed opportunity, especially here in the dawning of the Age of Engagement.

Instead, most organizations either are oblivious to or do not care about the health and well-being of their people.

Nothing says an organization does not care about its providers more than when it fails to:

- Educate the physicians on burnout.
- Survey them on their major stressors.
- Work to proactively address their concerns.

Organizational Stress Relief ACTION STEPS

Work within your physician leadership structure to persuade your organization to:

- Fund and deliver burnout prevention training to all providers and staff.
- Survey your providers at least yearly with a set of questions that give you actionable information on lowering stress in the workplace.
- Create, fund, and support a Burnout Prevention Working Group.
- Use the survey results to identify a project that will have a stress lowering impact.
- Lead the project, growing your physician leaders on the way.
- Repeat the steps above.
- Journal on your experience.

For a complete overview of the Physician Engagement Formula and to learn how this structure could benefit you and your organization, use this page to contact us directly: ***www.thehappymd.com/contact.***

QUADRANT IV: ORGANIZATIONAL RECHARGE

"We are human beings, not human doings."
—Zen saying

*"There is virtue in work and there is virtue in rest.
Use both and overlook neither."*
—Alan Cohen

THIS SECTION IS taken from the *Burnout Prevention Matrix Report*, which contains over 117 ways physicians and organizations can work together to prevent burnout. Get your free copy of the full report in the Power Tools Library on the web at *www.thehappymd.com/powertools*.

Normalize the expectation of work-life balance

As part of the organizational commitment to health and wellness for the physicians and staff, there is a parallel commitment and expectation that physicians and staff will have a full life outside of their careers. This is the basis for the institutional support of part-time practice, reasonable vacation allowances, and sabbaticals.

Methods to improve the work-life balance include:

- Sabbatical privileges built into standard employment contract after a set amount of time
  - Onsite Programs
  - Onsite exercise facilities and exercise classes
  - Walking groups at lunch
  - Onsite massage and guided imagery library
  - Onsite programs to teach healthcare stress management and burnout prevention
  - Onsite programs to teach and allow the practice of mindfulness, meditation, and other stress relief tools (yoga, Tai Chi, etc.) to physicians and staff during work days
- Organization-centered social activities, parties, charity events, and onsite clubs

- Organizational participation in community charity activities with physicians and staff invited to participate
  - When you participate, you are representing your organization to the larger community and connecting with staff and colleagues outside the workplace.
  - It can be a refreshing change from the office or hospital environment.
  - You can connect in different ways with your colleagues, staff, their families, and your patients.
  - It is a chance to bear witness to the larger good you are doing in your town.
- Offsite tours and excursions for the physicians and staff sponsored by the organization
- Establishing and supporting a "culture of caring"
  - Establish the expectation that physicians check in with your partners and colleagues about how they are doing
  - Help partners get support if it appears to be needed, without stigma
  - Share outside interests

NOTE: Success indicators for a "culture of caring" are *yes* answers in your surveys to the following questions from the book *First Break all the Rules* by Marcus Buckingham and Curt Coffman:

- Does someone at work seem to care about me as a person?
- Is there someone at work who encourages my development?
- In the last seven days, have I received praise or recognition for good work?

Organizational Recharge ACTION STEPS

Look at the list of Quadrant IV options above and pick one to explore, experiment with, or launch in your organization. All of these can be fun, creative, out of the box experiences.

NOTE: You are probably being called to be a leader here as well. If these things are not happening in your organization right now, they are not likely to appear spontaneously anytime soon. These are recharge-enhancing ideas that require the breath of life from a willing and enthusiastic leader. If that is you, what plate will you spin up first?

Journal on your experience.

CHAPTER 5

NO ONE IS AN ISLAND

Leadership and Communication Skills for Physicians

"Coming together is a beginning.
Keeping together is progress.
Working together is success."
—Henry Ford

"None of us is as smart as all of us."
—Ken Blanchard

TEAM LEADERSHIP SKILLS FOR PHYSICIANS

As you begin to build your Ideal Practice, you will quickly notice how damaging Lone Ranger programming can be. No one is an island. There is no way you can possibly reach your practice goals without the help of your team. This is equally true at home.

Even if you decided to let go of the Lone Ranger and learn how to lead your team more effectively, you are still at a disadvantage because of how you learned to lead in your training. Here is what you were taught to do:

- Figure out everything all by yourself
- Give everyone else orders

That's not a very functional way to lead people, unless you really liked your drill sergeant in basic training.

Let me show you how this built-in leadership paradigm sets you up to work way too hard and never really get the best ideas out on the table before you take action. It is a recipe for struggle that is hidden in the way a doctor is taught to lead a team. You must expose and reprogram your leadership skills to share the work of building your Ideal Practice with your team.

When this is done well, your team and family will be key allies in your success and happy to play their role from the start.

WHEN THE LONE RANGER WORKS...
AND WHEN IT DOESN'T

As we pass through the seven to seventeen years of our medical education, we gradually and inevitably inherit the role of king or queen of the clinical care team. We are expected to lead because of our specialized skills and knowledge base. Our position at the head of the clinical care team is automatic and unquestioned once we are board certified.

Along the way, we also inherit a leadership style that will radically compromise your ability to create your Ideal Practice unless we expose it here and now.

We learn to be the classic top-down, command-and-control leader. This style is audible in the language we use to describe how a doctor relates to the team.

The doctor "gives orders," and the team (and patient) is expected to obey or comply.

This unconscious and universal leadership style has negative consequences for everyone involved:

- The doctor works too hard.
- You feel like you have to know all the answers and that asking for help is a sign of weakness.
- The team is turned into "sheep" waiting for the doctor to tell them what to do. They are waiting for orders and hesitate to act without a direct command.
- Much of the skills and experience of your team go to waste. You don't ask what they think, they don't volunteer their opinions without being asked, and poor decisions are made and acted on all the time.

This Lone Ranger/top-down style is inherent in the structure of the medical team, because it works well in the area of clinical diagnosis and treatment. The doctor makes the diagnosis and supervises/leads the treatment team via orders. That's great...but...

What about all the other activities that go into the day-to-day functioning of your patient care team and your larger organization—the basics of patient flow, administration, operations, and personnel issues? Your team will see you as the leader and look to you to give them orders, even in these non-clinical areas where—in reality—you really don't know what you are talking about. The person giving orders (you) often turns out to be the least-qualified member of the team to comment on the subject at hand.

Example:

How often does a member of your team or your practice manager come to you with a question about operations? Something like, "Dr. Smith, what should we do about these pathology reports? I just found a pile of them in Dr. Jones's box by mistake."

How should you know? You spend your day in the room with patients. You don't know what is going on outside the exam room and don't have a clue about what to do with the path reports. You are one of the last people who should be asked to answer that question.

That won't stop you from giving it a shot, though.

There you sit at the apex of the top-down physician leadership pyramid. This is not going to end well if you are the Lone Ranger who tries to answer this question intelligently, but everyone is waiting for you to tell them what to do. You will give an answer/order, they will obey/comply, and it will take three or four tries to get a system that works. This happens every day in doctors' offices around the world. It does not have to be this way.

Notice:

These operational issues are the exact problems that drive you crazy during your workday and get in the way of you actually practicing medicine. If all you had to do was see patients, diagnose, and build treatment plans, you would be in doctor heaven—at least that is everyone's fantasy.

Reality Check

To build your Ideal Practice, you must use your entire team. You must switch out the Lone Ranger for a true Team Captain. Your leadership must extend beyond your purely clinical activities and into non-clinical areas like patient flow and the flow of documentation.

You and your team must excel at all the activities that take place while you are in the room with the patient. This is different than giving orders.

Excellence in your entire practice takes a different leadership skill set. No more king or queen or top-down Lone Ranger.

THE TEAM CAPTAIN

Let me show you a whole different collaborative physician leadership style I call the "Team Captain." This leadership style is one where:

- You don't have to work so hard.
- You tap the skills and experiences of your whole team—they come up with the answers, because they are the experts in operations.
- The whole team is engaged and enthusiastic from the start.

There are just three simple steps to help you let go of your Lone Ranger. Let me show you the steps and give you an example of what they look like in action.

Three Steps to the Team Captain

1. Set and Hold the Vision/Goal

This is one of Steven Covey's "seven habits of highly effective people." As he says, "Begin with the end in mind."

One of the Team Captain's most important skills is setting the Vision and giving the team an outcome Goal. In the example of the misplaced path reports above, the target could be:

Get all the path reports filed appropriately within twenty-four hours of receiving them.

Setting the vision/goal frames the team discussion from this point forward. This goal keeps everyone on target, moving to your vision of success.

2. Ask Powerful Questions

This is another skill set we didn't learn in med school or residency. The ability to ask powerful, open-ended questions is key to the Team Captain physician leadership style.

The simplest way to ensure your questions are always open-ended is to start them with either:

"What . . ."

Or

"How . . ."

A question beginning with *what* or *how* can't be answered with a yes or no. When faced with this kind of a question, the listener must think first and then answer with a complete thought. (These are fabulous questions for your patient interviews as well.)

These questions are the foundation for tapping into your team's skills and experience.

Power Tip:

You can also use these questions to identify the Vision/Goal with your team. That's right; you can really let go of your Lone Ranger when you understand Power Questions. You can even use them to help your team brainstorm your Vision for the project. It could sound like this:

"We have been having some trouble getting charts filed accurately and in a timely manner.
Let's do something about this. Before we get started I would like to ask:
WHAT is our Vision for what success looks like here?
HOW will we know we are being successful?"

When your team takes part in setting the Vision/Goals that organize their work, they are bought in from the start. You can relax into managing the discussion rather than trying to figure it out all by yourself.

---

3. Listen and Hold the Problem Solving Context

As the Team Captain, you are responsible for creating and maintaining the *context* in which your *team* solves the *team's* problems. Your job is to create and maintain a team environment where people collaborate and cooperate, working together to solve the team's problems—rather than waiting for you to give orders.

To accomplish this as a physician leader, you must . . .

- Hold the Vision: "Remember everyone, our Vision of success here is all test reports filed within twenty-four hours."
- Ask Powerful Questions—Starting with "What" or "How"
  - "What are your thoughts on how we can make that happen?"
  - "How would you suggest we change the way we do things now?"
- Lead the discussion with questions, rather than giving orders. This maintains the environment of collaboration.
  - Be open to everyone's input.
  - Use the best ideas on the table, no matter where they came from.

Trusting your team and engaging them from the start is the essence of Team Captain leadership. Powerful Questions are the key tool that will make all the difference.

Remember, *you* don't have to come up with all the answers.

Figuring out all the answers and giving orders is the Lone Ranger. Go ahead and let him go. When you are that kind of top-down physician leader, you are working too hard.

With these new Team Captain leadership skills, you will begin to notice something very interesting. This realization flies in the face of everything you were taught about being a top-down leader.

You don't need all the answers if you have:

- A Vision
- Powerful Questions
- A Team

Power Tip:

Now, you will have your own ideas on solutions. You and I both know that. Just remember, if this is not a purely clinical issue—if it has anything to do with patient flow or things that go on outside the exam room when you are with a patient—you are not the most qualified person on the team.

The Team Captain's goal is simple: get the best ideas out on the table by tapping the skills and experience of every single member of your team.

You lead the discussion using your Powerful Questions.

Save your ideas until last.

Add your input only at the end, and see if it adds to the discussion. If your ideas work, and the team agrees, use them. If someone else has a better suggestion, use that idea. Whatever you do, don't just wade in and give orders from the start. This will shut your team down and leave you with only a fraction of the value your team could bring with a more collaborative context.

Example #1

Team Problem Solving

Let's use the case of the misfiled path reports above. Here is what a Team Captain, a collaborative physician leader, might do with this issue.

You discuss the problem with your practice manager and agree the goal is to have the path reports all filed correctly within twenty-four hours of them being delivered.

You pull the entire team together (your monthly staff meeting is ideal for this). Lead the meeting off with something like this:

> *We have had some issues with getting path reports filed appropriately and in a timely fashion. Going forward, our goal as a team is to figure out a way to get all path reports filed correctly within twenty-four hours of them being delivered to the office.*
>
> *I am not the expert here and want us to design this system as a team.*
> *We need everyone's input to build a system that works for all of us.*

Start Asking Powerful Questions:

- What are your thoughts on how we could get these path reports filed?
- How do you suggest we approach this issue?
- What are the things we are doing now that seem to work at least a little bit?
- How can we do more of these?
- What things are not working?
- How can we change them to hit our goal?
- What members of our team need to be involved in this new system?
- How can we make this so it involves as few people and as few touches of paper as possible?
- How can we make it so this path report filing system does not interfere with the activities of caring for our patients?
- How will we track the performance of this new system?
- What is our next step?
- Who is the manager of this project?
- When will we meet to discuss this again?

In a short period of time, your team will design this system. You don't have to have the answers. You have the Powerful Questions and focus them on the Vision/ Goal of your ideal outcome.

Because the team was involved in designing the system from the start, they are fully bought in and engaged. They don't have to obey an order from you. They are carrying out an action plan they helped create. Creating this action plan tapped the skills and experience of the whole team.

Goodbye, Lone Ranger. Hello, Team Captain.

Example #2:

The Effective Monthly Team Meeting

Ideally, your Team Captain skill set is on full display in your monthly staff meetings. I know the monthly staff meeting is often disrespected and ineffective. Most of the time, this is simply because of the poor facilitation and leadership skills of the person in charge. You skip your monthly staff meeting at your peril for one simple reason:

You must *work on* your practice, not just *in* it.

If you don't take time to step out of the flow of the way you do things now—as a complete team—and work on improving your current systems, things will never improve. You will be putting out one fire after another. You must work *on* your practice, not just *in* your practice, to make progress toward your Ideal Practice Description. If utilized properly, your monthly team meeting is the best way to encourage your team to help you get there.

Try these steps:

- Have a basket where you and your team members can put suggestions, problems, and questions during the office day. The contents of this basket are the raw materials for your staff meeting.
- At the meeting, run through the items in the basket. This is another form of batch processing.
- Help your team prioritize and pick *one* (plate spinning) issue to work on.
- Ask Powerful Questions.
- Come to consensus on your Vision of what success looks like when you address this challenge.
- Use Powerful Questions to gather the best ideas for action steps.
- Continue to use Powerful Questions to generate a realistic action plan.
- Kick your action plan into gear.
- Follow up on this project at your next meeting.

Power Tip:
Normally, the basket of topics for your monthly staff meeting will only contain items the team members see as a problem. You can expand your team's ability to make rapid positive changes by asking a couple more Power Questions:
- What is not working, and how can we fix it?
- What *is* working, and how can we do more of it?
- What can we stop doing?
- What can we start doing that we don't do now?
- What else?

Switching to Team Captain and Power Questions will dramatically improve your effectiveness as a leader.

These simple skills are always applicable, from your monthly staff meeting to the boardroom of a Fortune 100 corporation. In fact, these so called "soft skills" are the foundation of any effective leader's toolbox. They are typically not covered in formal leadership education such as an MBA program, even in this depth.

TEAM CAPTAIN LEADERSHIP SUMMARY

You don't need all the answers when you have:

- A Vision
- Powerful Questions
- A Team

As the Team Captain, you must:

- Hold the Vision (you can ask questions to generate the Vision, too).
- Ask Powerful Questions starting with "what" or "how."
- Lead the discussion with questions, rather than giving orders.

Team Captain Leadership ACTION STEPS

- Look at your Ideal Practice Description and Master Plan
- When you have decided what plate you will spin up first . . .
  - ‣ How can you help your team help you?
  - ‣ When is your first team meeting where you will introduce this topic?
  - ‣ What is your initial Vision of a successful outcome?

ADDITIONAL RESOURCES IN THE POWER TOOLS LIBRARY

- The Team Problem Solving Protocol
- Mini-training on the complete question set to create a complete improvement project

Access these free web resources at this link: ***www.thehappymd.com/powertools***.

HOW TO MANAGE YOUR BOSS

HERE IN 2014—WHERE employed physicians are projected to comprise half of the workforce by 2021—autonomy has become a quaint, old-fashioned memory.

Within the bureaucracy of a large healthcare organization, you are no longer in charge of your practice environment. You are now positioned firmly in the middle of a large organizational chart with layers of bosses above you. This person often has a frustrating ability to dictate the specifics of your practice, unless you figure out a way to have some influence on their decisions.

Let me show you three keys to managing your boss if you are an employed physician. These are the tools you need to make them an ally in creating your Ideal Practice.

Have you ever asked yourself this question?

"If I am not the boss anymore, how do I manage the person who is?"

As an employed physician, you will quickly realize you no longer sit at your historical position atop the organizational chart. These days, you have a boss above you. Sometimes, this person is not even a physician.

This is not a situation where you simply keep your head down and learn how to deal with your frustrations more effectively. You must somehow manage this person if you are going to find any wiggle room to create your Ideal Practice.

Like it or not, the quality of your relationship with your boss is a huge factor in your quality of life.

- A good relationship can provide you with a powerful advocate for your Ideal Practice.
- A poor relationship with your immediate supervisor can lead to burnout and is one of the top three reasons employed physicians quit their jobs.

THREE KEYS TO MANAGING YOUR BOSS

1. Understand Your Boss X2

It is vitally important to understand your boss on two key levels:

a. Know His or Her Personality and Communication Style

Is your boss an action-oriented person who wants the bullet points before making a quick decision, or a detail-oriented, introverted "engineer type" who requires all the information and a good chunk of time to decide how to proceed? Or, someone completely different?

Study your boss and his or her communication style very carefully. Pretend you are an anthropologist, carefully observing your boss as a key member of your "tribe."

- How does he schedule his days?
- How does he prefer to be communicated with—email, text, phone, or in-person?
- How do the people who have the best working relationships with your boss relate to this person? What success factors can you identify and emulate?

Then, practice the Platinum Rule: "Treat people how they want to be treated."

Match your boss's communication style and personality when the two of you are together. Give him the information and time he wants, just the way he wants it, especially when you are making a request for change to your work structure.

b. Know Your Boss's Goals and Priorities

Your boss almost certainly has a boss. She has her own personal set of goals and orders from above.

Do you know what her priorities/goals/objectives are? The easiest way to find this out is to ask her directly and take good notes. It will be much easier for you to get what you need from your boss if your request aligns with one of her own goals. This is the essence of a win-win solution.

- What are her key objectives for this quarter and this year?
- What role does she see you playing in reaching these goals?

2. Understand Yourself X2

You must understand yourself on these same two levels.

a. What is your personality and communication style and how does it differ from your boss's?

Notice the way you communicate naturally and how that either matches or conflicts with your boss's personality and style. In most cases, you will need to modify the way you communicate to connect effectively with your boss.

Remember, you are striving for the Platinum Rule here. *Treat people the way they want to be treated.* So, if your boss likes all the details and time to consider his decision, give him just what he wants: details and time.

b.) What are your goals and needs?

If you have created your Ideal Practice Description and are using your Master Plan to continuously improve your practice, you will probably have requests for your boss every month.

Winning your boss's support is often the key to making the practice changes you require. Your Master Plan helps you pinpoint exactly how you need your boss to contribute to your success.

- Do your best to align your needs with one of his goals and create the win-win that pleases both of you.
- Then, ask for what you want.

You may need to negotiate back and forth and be willing to accept a bit of a compromise. Do not let that stop you from being clear on what you want and then asking for it.

3. Manage Your Relationship

Let's face it—you can't actually manage your boss. You are not in the position in the org chart for that. What you can manage is the relationship between you. Most physicians miss this point altogether. Here's how that relationship usually works.

You see your boss only a couple times a year, and most often that is when she is sitting in your office to tell you there is a problem.

That is actually the absence of a relationship.

You can't manage a vacuum. The chance of you getting something you need from your boss when this is the nature of your relationship is close to zero.

You must manage the relationship proactively. Think of it this way: your relationship is another example of an energetic bank account. This time the energy it holds is *trust*.

Every positive interaction makes a deposit of trust and goodwill into this account. You will need a balance of trust to draw on if there is a conflict or problem. If you only see your boss when she stops by to tell you about something that is not working, you have nothing to draw on. No matter what the exact conversation is about, it will drive the two of you even farther apart.

BUILDING TRUST WITH YOUR BOSS

Have regular collegial meetings with your boss to make sure you are on the same page. Make trust deposits in these meetings so your relationship has something to draw on when you need it.

How often should you meet? Once a month like clockwork is very helpful. Once a quarter is a bare minimum. Your objective is to get to know him and his goals and let him know your goals and challenges.

Here are some questions to ask:

- What are your goals for this quarter and this year?
- What role do you see me playing in those goals?
- How else can I help you get there?
- How do you evaluate my performance, and what are the most important numbers for you?
- How am I doing at this time?
- What do you see as ways I can improve?
- What is something you see on the horizon that I can start preparing for now?

Down the road, these are also the conversations where you can ask for what you need to keep creating your Ideal Practice.

Keep working to make deposits in your relationship bank account with your boss. Shoot for a ratio of positive 5:1, meaning five positive interactions to every one negative or uncomfortable one. This way, your Trust Account with your boss will always be in positive territory.

Don't be a whiner!

The typical physician will point to a problem and ask the boss, "What are you going to do about this?" Notice this is a classic phrase a victim uses. It is complaining, pure and simple. It is incredibly common, and it will destroy your relationship and make you adversaries immediately. You will blow any chance of your boss helping you create your Ideal Practice if you communicate with him in this fashion.

This doesn't mean you can't ask your boss for help with the problems you are facing. However, if you change your communication just a little bit, you will bring your boss into a position of being your ally rather than your biggest frustration. Here is a rule to follow:

*Any time you bring your boss a problem, **always** bring a solution, too.*

You are a problem solver. It only takes a little more effort to think of a solution or two before you go talk to your boss. You are also able to see the difference between a problem and a dilemma; your boss probably doesn't understand this distinction. You can teach him the difference. This allows you to shift from being just another whining doctor to the two of you working on an effective strategy as a team.

Ideally, your solution/strategy is a win-win that accomplishes two things at once:

1. It gives you more of what you want.
2. It meets one of your boss's objectives at the same time.

Remember the "Continuation Rule"

Every interaction you have with your boss (or any other person for that matter) sets the stage for your next encounter.

- If you end on a positive note, your next meeting will continue on that same positive trajectory—even if your discussion is about a problem.
- If the meeting ends badly, you will start the next one in the pits as well.
- Do everything you can to avoid ending any meeting in a negative fashion.

Managing your boss ACTION STEPS

1. Figure out who your boss is.

This may be a challenge in your organization, especially if your structure has changed recently. If you know who your boss is, skip to step #2. If not, make sure you find out who the organization sees as your immediate supervisor.

Is it your CMO, someone in the administration, your practice manager, the chairperson of your executive committee? Figure out who in the organization you report to, and then do step two.

2. Begin to observe your boss closely and take notes.

Prepare yourself to begin practicing the Platinum Rule. Know how your boss communicates and makes decisions.

Arrange a meeting in the absence of any problems or crisis.

Call up your boss and tell her something like this:

I would like to buy you a cup of coffee and get to know your goals for me—and the larger organization—so we are always on the same page.

I would like to be a better team player.

I know you are a very important member of the team here, and I would like to see how we can each do a better job of supporting each other.

When can we get together?

Let her determine the place and time; then, get to work on your specific question list for the conversation.

3. Create your list of questions.

The complete list of questions I recommend is in the Manage Your Boss Worksheet in the Power Tools Library here: *www.thehappymd.com/powertools.*

4. Hold the meeting, keep it real, and take great notes.

- Make sure that your conversation adds to your relationship Trust Account while being real about your concerns. This may be your first collegial interaction, so do not ask for any changes just yet.
- Set yourself a goal to increase your knowledge base about your boss's personality, leadership, decision-making style, and goals/objectives.
- Get to know your boss as a person, too. Does he have children, outside interests, or hobbies? Where do the two of you have common ground?
- Take great notes, just like you would with a patient. Always be adding to your knowledge base and building your relationship.

5. Schedule your next meeting.

Make a habit of scheduling your next visit with your boss before this one is done, so you always have a relationship-building meeting on the books with him before you walk out the door. Quarterly is great. Monthly or every other month is better. Ideally, you should put the whole year's worth of meetings on your calendars at once before this first one is over.

6. Keep your Ideal Practice Description and Master Plan up to date.

Know the latest version of your Ideal Practice Description and Master Plan. Keep track on the action steps that require your boss's assistance and support.

7. Build a win-win, and ask for it.

Pick the highest priority change you want to make to your practice. Look at it from two perspectives: yours *and* your boss's. Put yourself in your boss's shoes now that you know more about him and his situation.

Your boss will most likely have two concerns you do not share: manpower and money. Put yourself in his shoes and you will see them immediately. As you build a win-win solution/strategy, make sure you have taken into account the additional manpower and expense of what you are suggesting.

If you have a way to mitigate for these concerns, give your boss your suggestions immediately.

If you don't have a clear idea of how to acquire the people and the budget for your suggestion upfront, acknowledge that and get your boss to brainstorm options with you.

Do your best to create a solution that will be a *win* for *both* of you. Prepare to present this request at your next meeting.

8. Rehearse your conversation.

Never, ever go into these conversations cold. Brainstorm your boss's most likely questions and objections and prepare responses to them. Practice your responses in the mirror so you are prepared when you are face-to-face.

> ## Power Tip:
> Use your team here. Significant others can be the perfect people to play your boss in your rehearsals. They have heard your stories and often surprise physicians by giving an Oscar-worthy performance. They usually participate with gusto when invited to help you prepare for this conversation.

9. Be flexible and willing to negotiate.

Make sure you have a positive balance in your relationship Trust Account before you make any requests and that your last encounter with your boss was a positive one. Use the Squeegee Breath before and during your conversation to keep your cool. Engage in as much give and take as necessary to ensure your boss is aware of your flexibility.

10. Be patient.

Leaders and administrators do not have the same finely-tuned sense of urgency as a clinician. You may not reach a happy agreement in this first meeting. Don't accept an outright *no* at this point. Keep this as an ongoing discussion for future meetings. If you re-address this issue over time, you are likely to find new ideas that make it possible down the road. Do not give up if this is important to you. Apply your creativity, and stay in a relationship with your boss.

The Result

When my coaching clients apply these boss management skills, they are often surprised at the flexibility, support, and positive working relationship that results. In many cases, things you thought were impossible—like going to part-time or getting additional clerical support for your practice—are immediately available when you first put yourself in their shoes and then present a win-win request to your boss.

ADDITIONAL RESOURCES IN THE POWER TOOLS LIBRARY ON THE WEB

The Manage Your Boss Worksheet: Complete training on these "manage your boss" skills, including the full recommended question set for meeting with your immediate supervisor.

Access these free web resources at this link: *www.thehappymd.com/powertools*.

THE LEADERSHIP MASTER SKILL

How to say "Thank You" with impact

As you recover from burnout or move in the direction of your Ideal Practice, you will soon realize that your success hinges in large part on how you build and manage your teams. "No one is an island," and no physician is one either. You must have a team in the office or hospital and another one at home to be successful. It helps when they enjoy the experience of being on your team, too.

You have learned the Team Captain leadership paradigm. Now, let me show you what I consider to be the Master Skill of a quality Team Captain—how to say "thank you" with impact.

Effort vs. Skill

Research coming from parenting experts gives us a window into the most effective way to say thank you.[10] The two common patterns of thanks are to acknowledge a person's skill or a person's hard work. Here's how the two of them sound:
  - "You are very good at that. Thanks a lot. I really appreciate it."
  - "Thanks for your hard work. I really appreciate it."

Which one do you think is more effective? It is the acknowledgment of *effort*. If you are good at anything, it is because you have put in the hard work to hone your skills. When you say thanks, I encourage you to acknowledge effort.

Practice Until You are Comfortable

Many physicians say thank you very infrequently. It's that darn blind spot that keeps us focused on problems, errors, and the gap. Most of us are relatively awkward at doing it. So, let me give you some tips.

Short and Sweet

Pick a phrase that works for you, one that is short and to the point. For example, "Thanks for your hard work, I/the patient/the team really appreciate it." Then, practice it in the mirror until you are comfortable and it feels natural to you.

Catch Them Doing Something Right

Look for opportunities to catch your people doing a good job. Thank them right on the spot. Don't be afraid to acknowledge them in a public setting, within earshot of others.

- Square your posture to face them directly.
- Look them in the eye.
- Thank them and …
- Move on.

Well done.

Bonus:

Just so you know, you probably just delivered a triple whammy deposit into their Energy Accounts with this one simple act (see Chapter one).

How often should you thank your people?

Simple: whenever you see a reason to. Research shows that once a week is about right.[11] Now, I don't advise you make a checklist and thank everyone once a week whether they deserve it or not. That would take all the meaning and authenticity out of your gratitude. Be on the lookout for reasons to thank your people for their hard work, and you will see them every day. Then, don't hold back on saying thank you. We all know that without these people you would never get home.

THANK YOU SUMMARY

- Practice saying thank you until you are comfortable.
- Acknowledge effort and all progress.
- Catch your people doing something right.

Thank you ACTION STEPS

- Choose your thank you phrase(s).
- Practice them until you are comfortable.

- Be on the lookout for opportunities to thank your people for their effort and your team's progress toward your Ideal Practice.
- Who do you owe a thank you to right now?
- When will you thank them?
- Repeat the last two questions thinking about your "home team" and family.
- Journal about your experience.

ADDITIONAL RESOURCES IN THE POWER TOOLS LIBRARY ON THE WEB

- What to do when a patient says thank you
  - ‣ Complete training on how you can respond when a patient thanks you
  - ‣ How to turn this into a triple whammy Energy Account deposit for both of you

Access these free web resources at this link: ***www.thehappymd.com/powertools***.

CHAPTER 6

DO I HAVE TO CHANGE JOBS?

When to Leave and How to Find Your Ideal Job This Time Around

"There are risks and costs to action. But they are far less than the long range risks of comfortable inaction."
—John F. Kennedy

"Great minds have purposes, others have wishes."
—Washington Irving

I am frequently asked how often an actual job change is necessary to recover from burnout. Here is my experience.

If I meet a physician before they have made the decision to quit, about 70 percent end up staying put. They use their Ideal Practice Description and their Master Plan to reach enough overlap in their Venn of Happiness that they don't feel a need to move on. These three concepts create a framework for moving your current job more in alignment with your ideal job. Exactly how to increase the overlap of your Venn of Happiness is straightforward. You have the blueprint right in front of you. All you have to do is take the action steps required.

Whether or not you will need to change jobs depends upon your success implementing your Master Plan. If you can't get the overlap between this job and your Ideal Job up to a percentage you are comfortable with—for most physicians this is in the 60-95 percent range—changing job positions may be the answer.

For example, you may reach a point where you have used the tools in this book to make some changes over the course of several months. Let's say you notice your Venn of Happiness overlap increases from a baseline of 40 percent to its current position of 55 percent, and the improvement has stalled there. You consult your Ideal Practice Description and the remaining steps on your Master Plan and conclude this is as good as it is going to get in your current position.

Is that good enough to stay? You get to decide.

I have helped dozens of physicians find a new job position since the launch of ***TheHappyMD.com***. I am not a recruiter. I do not find a job for them. What we do is work together on a high quality job search using the same Ideal Practice Description you developed back in chapter three. Your IPD organizes your search efforts, the efforts of any recruiters you might work with, your interviews, and your ultimate decision process.

TWO PHYSICIAN JOB SEARCH MISTAKES YOU MUST AVOID

DANGER: I have worked with a number of burnout coaching clients who stepped right into these two job search traps. They usually contact me after changing jobs when the new job turns out to be even worse (often much worse) than the one they left behind. They literally jumped out of the frying pan and into the fire. Don't let this happen to you.

1. Do not quit this job.

I encourage you to stay put, keep your head down, use the Quadrant I stress relief tools in chapter four, and stay in your current position while you are looking for your new job. Once you have made the decision to leave, this job is now your bridge to that better future.

I learned this lesson the hard way. One of the most stressful things about my career-ending burnout was my decision to walk away. It felt like the only thing I could do at the time. You may feel the same way in your situation at this moment. I encourage you to make the decision to move on, but do not quit this job. Use it as a bridge, instead.

This advice is even more important if you are in a position of financial weakness. If you are in debt with a negative net worth and do not have at least enough savings for six months of your bills, staying put is imperative. Your financial situation will drive you to make decisions out of desperation, and you and everyone in your family will suffer.

If you implement the Squeegee Breath, the Schedule Hack, and the Boundary Ritual—adding in the BID Huddle and some batch processing (all in chapter four)—you will be able to stop the downward spiral in your energy while you conduct a high quality job search.

This job is your bridge to a better place.

You can use this job and its income as a bridge to a better position. This position can provide for you and your family while you identify and move to a job more aligned with your Ideal Practice Description. In order to ensure this move upward actually takes place, you must avoid the physician's job search mistake number two.

2. Do not search for a new job the same way you applied to medical school or residency.

If you do, your success in finding a better position in your search will rely purely on luck. Here is what I mean.

Most of us learn how to search for and obtain a new job position using the template of the methods we used to get into medical school and/or residency. Big mistake!

Remember back then. We were basically doing anything we could to get accepted. We were doing the interview equivalent of jumping up and down and shouting, "Pick me, pick me!" You were doing anything you could to get *them* to pick *you*.

That is *not* what this job search will be about.

In fact, a healthy job search turns the tables 180 degrees—it is another Mind Flip.

Turn the Tables

In your search for your next position, make sure this job is a better match with your Ideal Practice Description than where you are now.

- You are not trying to get *them* to pick *you*.
- You are working to figure out if *you* will pick *them*.

Remember the "out of the frying pan and into the fire" clients I mentioned above? The mistake they made was remaining focused on what they didn't like about their current position and running away from these problems. They focused on getting a new employer to pick them and jumped as soon as a job became available. They were rarely lucky enough to stumble into a situation that was a good match for their Ideal Practice Description.

A High Quality Job Search

A high quality job search relies on you being crystal clear about your Ideal Practice Description. With your IPD in hand, you can focus all your screening and interview efforts on finding a good match. Now *you* are screening *them*.

I have to repeat this because it is so important.

- You must know what you are looking for *first*.
- Ask the questions required to *screen them*…

- To see if they match your Ideal Practice Description…
- To decide if *you* will pick *them*.

In your job search, you will use your IPD to generate your interview question set and take those questions with you when you go on your site visit.

- When you return home, you can sit down and build the Venn of Happiness for this job opportunity.
- You will understand just how much overlap there is between this job and your Ideal Practice.
- Then, only one decision remains. Ask yourself, *Is this overlap enough to take this job?*

You are picking them at the end of a high quality job search focused on finding a better match with your Ideal Practice Description. In this case, there will be no jumping into the fire.

Now, you may worry about the fact that you are not working to get them to pick you. Let me be of some reassurance here. When you organize your job search and interview questions around your IPD, I have never had a client find a job they wanted to take where they were not offered the position. Most likely, you will be complimented on your preparation. Your awareness and focus will impress them, and you will get the contract.

There are a number of steps to a high quality job search. We have packaged them into a separate training: "Physician Job Search Secrets—Simple Steps to Finding Your Ideal Practice." You will find a link for more information on this program in the Power Tools Library on the web at ***www.thehappymd.com/powertools***.

CHAPTER 7

YOUR EXIT STRATEGY

Making Room For What Comes Next

"Life is no brief candle to me. It is a sort of splendid torch which I have got a hold of for the moment, and I want to make it burn as brightly as possible before handing it on to future generations."
—George Bernard Shaw

"The young man knows the rules, but the old man knows the exceptions."
—Oliver Wendell Holmes, Sr.

In a span of just four months in 2013, I met four physicians in four separate abusive work situations. Each came to me for coaching on how to recover from their well-earned burnout. They were all over sixty, had worked hard to build an impressive net worth, and were still in good health.

During our initial consultation, I asked each, "Why are you still working?"

Each time, the question was met by thirty seconds of silence and then a hushed, "I hadn't thought of that."

They were telling the truth. The option of *not* working had never entered their awareness. They were completely occupied by dealing with the day-to-day stresses of practice habits developed over thirty-plus years of medicine. The option of retirement was blatantly obvious to me, though invisible to them.

I encourage you to figure out your Exit Strategy from medicine now, so you don't miss it when you get there.

WHAT IS YOUR EXIT STRATEGY?

You might think of it this way:

- Your decision to become a physician opened a frame—the frame of what you hoped would be an extraordinary picture.
- You paint the picture from the bottom up, on purpose, from the palette of your

171

Ideal Practice, your Bucket List, and the family you will leave behind when you are gone.

- Your Exit Strategy completes the frame on this picture.
- Your Exit Strategy leaves you free to move on to your next art project, not simple retirement. This is a new frame on a new picture. I wonder what that vision is for you. Your Exit Strategy closes this frame and invites the next picture to form.

For most, your Exit Strategy is triggered by a financial threshold.

As much as we might hold our career as a calling, an art, and a science, when you no longer need to work to make the money to support your lifestyle, you cross a very significant threshold. This is a place where you are financially free. When you cross this threshold, you work because you *want* to, not because you *have* to. If you don't want to practice anymore, you don't have to.

Know Your Number

If a significant portion of your Exit Strategy is reaching a financial goal, I encourage you to put some concrete numbers on that goal now. Whether you are just starting in your practice or have been working as a physician for thirty years, know the exact net worth number you are using as your target. Regularly check your progress toward your goal.

Hire a financial planner, and meet with him or her once a year. Know your goals and your progress toward them. This is another place where you can acknowledge and celebrate your progress. Treat yourself like a dog for any progress toward your target net worth. You deserve it.

Financial questions are a core component of my initial conversation with doctors. A fascinating component of those consults is how infrequently a physician knows their net worth. Most of the time, they are afraid to know the actual number. They fear they are not saving adequately and would rather not know at all than be disappointed.

For the majority of my clients, one of my first recommendations is that they visit a financial planner and begin using him or her as one of their trusted advisors going forward. For almost all who follow that recommendation, they are surprised when their net worth is finally calculated. Eight times out of ten, they are actually doing better than expected.

For some, they realize their Exit Strategy has arrived. They can close the frame, celebrate all the experiences and lessons learned on the journey, and move on.

RETIREMENT HEAD TRASH

For most physicians, a whole new flavor of head trash comes up at the mention of retirement. Let's name it now so you can recognize, get rid of it, and make some room for a fresh, new, retired version of you.

<u>A common voice in your head says, "I don't want to stop being a doctor."</u>

I have news for you: you never stop being a doctor. Your worldview, your skills and experience, the letters after your name …they never go away. You will be a doctor until your last breath—trust me on this.

Fortunately, your physician instincts are a universal skill set in the non-medical world. You are superb at finding the unifying diagnosis and prescribing an appropriate treatment for almost any problem in almost any setting. If you sit on the PTA at your children's school, volunteer as a medical missionary, or someone asks you to be on the board of a local company, the organization is richer for having you there. Your doctor-ness adds to the discussion. You will find people seek out your opinion because of the value your physician's perspective brings to the discussion.

<u>Another common voice says something like, "What would I do with myself? I would just get bored."</u>

I say balderdash. That's just head trash. Bored is a choice. Now, you get to reset your self-worth to match the quality of your time rather than the quantity of your actions.

There is an adjustment period, for sure. There will be months of adjusting to being in complete charge of your schedule. You will find a way to make a contribution to your family and community that matches your sense of purpose in medicine. You will also find new activities capable of holding your passion and enthusiasm once your practice is not dominating your time and energy.

All of a sudden, it is as if that 800-pound gorilla has been sent to a wildlife farm in the country and you have your "house" all to yourself again. It takes a little getting used to, and you can handle it.

<u>An Ideal Retirement Description is in order</u>

Just like the Ideal Practice Description can be used to become much more on purpose about your career, you can build an Ideal Retirement Description and use it in exactly the same way.

Even if you are not practicing, you can continue to use your weekly strategy session to build a more ideal life here in your next phase. There is never a bad time to live your life on purpose. Now, you have much more bandwidth and time available to you to practice these skills and smile as you reap the benefits.

The energy of contentment

Before we end this chapter on your Exit Strategy, let me share the following observation about slowing down. I want to tell you something that I hope gives you confidence as you contemplate letting go of your identity as a practicing physician.

I have found this to be true in my life. Check it out and see if you notice it too.

When I was practicing, there was always a certain frantic energy to seeing patients. No matter how smooth the day went, unexpected things would pop up. We swam in a constant stream of busyness. Things stacked up and we worked through them. We got behind, and we caught up. People approached from all directions to ask a question or get an opinion. It felt good to be the center of attention. There was a certain satisfaction in getting the work done. It was a high frequency buzz of being productive and plowing through the work.

If someone had asked me in that moment, "Are you happy?" it would have seemed a silly question to me. I was busy, productive, and getting the work done. Happiness had nothing to do with it. I was at work.

It was quite addictive, though.

If the work slowed down below a certain threshold, I felt unproductive. I would look for things to do rather than just sit around. Guilt would creep in around the edges. I was "jonesing" to be busy.

Fast forward to after I quit my practice.

My days were no longer ruled by my patients and my schedule. It took a while to let go of the hunger to be productive and do lots of things. I missed people coming to me and asking all sorts of questions. I realized that I was sometimes doing things just to keep busy.

One early morning as I was journaling with a cup of coffee, a pleasant and slightly strange feeling came over me. I automatically put down my cup, smiled, and cocked my head to the side like a dog when it doesn't understand what it is looking at. Something subtle was trying to get my attention, as if it was using a back door to my awareness.

It was a sense of satisfaction, similar to the one of having a productive day at the office …only on a completely different wavelength. This was quieter, lower frequency, calm and relaxed. I could breathe into it to make it more vivid in my awareness. Still, it took me several minutes to recognize its essence. This was happiness. This was contentment.

As I wrote in my journal, I realized up until now I had always hoped to construct this feeling by working hard enough, seeing enough patients, making enough money, and being a good doctor. I had been conditioned to believe happiness is something I earned or I put together piece by piece. If I was busy enough, productive enough, and brought home enough, I would end up being happy, too. What all this activity earned me was the satisfaction of being productive.

This feeling was very different.

It did not require effort. In fact, it appeared to be something that was present in the background of my awareness all the time. I had to step away from my practice and slow down for several months to be able to feel it clearly.

It was not a total stranger, though. I recognized it as something I had felt in fleeting moments during my practice—on a quiet weekend when I was not on call or on the last few days of a vacation.

Now, in the relative peace of being a doctor who is no longer in practice, this feeling is available full flow, straight from the tap, any time I want.

Check this out for yourself in a quiet moment.

Do you feel it? Is happiness and contentment there for you in the background? I encourage you to take a deep breath and invite it to sit a while with you. One way to invite it in is to practice the Satisfaction Mind Flip (chapter two) and count your blessings.

Right now, you can practice breathing and relaxing into the things that are going right in your life. Get familiar with the energy of happiness and contentment so you recognize it when it tries to get your attention.

Last but not least, I want you to know that much more of this feeling is available when you activate your Exit Strategy by stepping away from your practice and into your next phase. Here, you will have the space, time, and energy to become very familiar with happiness again—just like you were when you were a child.

You can relax and stop trying to earn it.

You will cock your head like a curious dog and then smile when you have finally slowed down enough to realize it is all around you, even now.

Exit Strategy ACTION STEPS

- Consult a financial advisor, and create your retirement plan.
- Visit your financial advisor once a year to measure and celebrate your progress.
- Know when you cross the threshold, and understand at that point that you only work now because you want to, not because you have to.
- Create an Ideal Retirement Description and review it at least monthly.
- Use weekly Strategy Sessions (with a cup of tea on a Sunday morning, perhaps) and your Ideal Retirement Description to create a new and beautiful picture in this next phase of your life.
- Practice the Satisfaction Mind Flip now to recognize happiness and contentment and develop the habit of noticing it all around you.
- Journal on your experience.

CHAPTER 8

CASE STUDIES

The following case studies illustrate how seven physicians, in very different circumstances, managed to create a more ideal life and ideal practice for themselves. My intention is to show you the universal nature of the tools above and the variety of ways they can be put to productive use.

AN UNEXPECTED RETIREMENT: DR. D

Dr. D was a fifty-nine-year old neurologist who came to me with a practice satisfaction level of 4 out of 10. She was overwhelmed with her volume of patients and friction amongst her partners. She was looking for assistance in going part-time, hoping that would give her relief from her obvious burnout. She hoped to work until she was sixty-four, although it was not clear why she had chosen that number.

I always ask financial questions in my first call with a client for a very simple reason. The state of your finances will dramatically affect your decision making. Desperate finances make for desperate choices. If you have socked away a nest egg, you have more flexibility and more choices available at any given time.

In addition, burnout does not discriminate based on your net worth. I have worked with doctors with net worth estimates from less than $500,000 to ones worth as high as $7 million. Burnout can knock physicians at both ends of this spectrum out of their practice with equal gusto.

In our first call, it became clear that Dr. D was financially free. In addition, her husband—also a physician—was seventy at the time, with multiple health issues that made it difficult to get around. Despite this, he was also still practicing medicine full-time.

Dr. D's initial call to me was prompted by an uncontrolled sobbing episode on a recent vacation. She was nearly incapable of contemplating returning to work. The realization was overwhelming. She was completely exhausted. She had her annual performance review with her boss coming up the next week and wanted to know how to speak with him to be able to go to part-time work.

When I suggested retirement might be the best option, she admitted she and her husband had plenty of items on their BIG Bucket List, including foreign travel, that they simply did not have time to get to do. I pointed out that if they did not retire soon, her husband was at significant risk of dying before he retired and she might end up taking those trips alone in the future.

We focused on a successful transition to retirement from that point forward.

Within five months, Dr. D was retired and vacationing with her husband in Greece. With her taking the lead, her husband retired three months later. They have cleaned decades of junk out of their home, completely redecorated, are back in shape, and are planning a trip to Wales next.

Dr. D's retirement transition was not without significant stress. Guilt at leaving her patients and her partners—a normal reaction—was something she had to come to grips with. She had served through a long productive career and didn't need to prove anything to anyone. It also helped when she realized it was her organization's responsibility to provide adequate care for the patients. I reminded her that she was not leaving anyone behind. The organization could have a locum tenens provider in her place in a matter of days. However, they wouldn't plan for those things until she put in her notice.

Another big stress Dr. D faced—a universal one when a doctor retires—is what to say to your colleagues, staff, and patients. They will ask you if you are okay, or if they did anything to upset you, hundreds of times after you put in your notice. We created and practiced her "talk track" multiple times, greatly reducing the stress of these conversations. "I am retiring to spend more time with my husband and my family. I am way overdue."

In hindsight, Dr. D realized that retirement was literally a lifesaving maneuver. If they had not stepped away, her husband might have "dropped dead at work." Now that they are free to workout, both of them recognize how de-conditioned they were and how it affected their overall health.

Dr. D would make sure younger physicians understand four things:

1. Blaming, justifying, and complaining are not useful coping mechanisms. Find some time to slow down to examine your thinking and focus on changing what is not working.
2. Understand that taking care of you is taking care of your patients.
3. Learn how to schedule in personal time in your week to recharge your energy banks.

4. When you are planning a significant change, have a coach or friend to keep you accountable to yourself. It helps a lot.

The most valuable concepts for her were:

- The Energetic Bank Accounts.
- Stepping out of the Victim and taking action instead.
- "Treat yourself like a dog" and patting herself on the back for each step.
- Working with their financial planner to transition from their salaries to retirement income.

Dr. D rates her satisfaction with life now at 8/10. She and her husband are still in the midst of adjusting to retirement, just six months out. I asked her, "What is the one thing you notice about being retired that you did not expect retirement to hold for you when you were still working?"

Here is her response:

Hard to just come up with 'one' thing, but perhaps just a profound sense of relief, a feeling that, thank God, it's over! I don't have to do that anymore.

From the pressures of premed studies, MCATs, and applying to schools; wondering if I would get in, med school studies, internship and residency, and twenty-five years of private practice—thirty-eight years, if you add it all up. I feel like I can finally relax and just be myself. I can't believe all of the things we put on hold, on the list to do someday, and, at last, someday is now!

The other word would be freedom. Each day, we have time to pursue activities of our choice. We've been spending an unbelievable amount of time reading and enjoying little luxuries such as enjoying coffee and breakfast in the morning, not having to rush around, cooking, and doing home projects. We love spending time with our two boys; we can take off whenever we want for a few days to see them. We have the emotional and spiritual energy to help them troubleshoot problems, or just hang out together at the beach.

LIFE BALANCE AND AN EMR STRATEGY: DR. B

When I first met Dr. B, his overlap with his Ideal Practice Description was a solid 70 percent. At the same time, he was feeling very challenged in two discreet areas: work-life balance and the pain of his documentation routine.

His wife was sick of his chronic frustration, of him getting home late with charts undone and not having enough energy to put into his marriage and three young children at home. Dr. B felt stuck in a system he didn't understand and had not been able to make significant changes to become more proactive. He has since made major changes in both who he is being and what he is doing at work.

The tools Dr. B finds most helpful are:

- A new EMR strategy. Dr. B carefully studied the native power users of EPIC in his practice. He found a "hidden master" of templates and "smart phrases", which lit a fire of belief that he could learn to do things differently. He has successfully automated the majority of his charting. He types less than 30 percent of his chart notes, leaves the office only twenty minutes after finishing with the last patient, and, 75 percent of the time, all of his charts are done.
- More effective leadership skills. Dr. B has worked diligently with his team, using powerful questions to ask for their help in reaching his goals. Together, they have changed his schedule with several thirty-minute blocks of time left unscheduled each day to maintain his flexibility. In their daily team huddles, they make a decision to book appointments at these times or keep them blocked.
- The Schedule Hack and intentional planning of family activities and family relationships. The self-reflection and proactive planning of his life outside of medicine has given him a new understanding of his relationships with his wife, family, and even his mother and siblings.
- How to manage and understand his boss. Dr. B's office is one of many in a large organization. He is actively managing his relationship with his superior. In the process, he has developed a new appreciation for why administrators do what they do and how to reach his personal goals within a bureaucracy.

Dr. B's current IPD overlap is 85 percent, and he feels his life is much more balanced. His advice for other doctors is:

> *You have to be careful to notice your idea about working harder does not always solve problems. Working smarter and being more effective with new tools and training is a key part of success.*
>
> *Realize the importance of balance from the outset. Balance family life, parenting, and work.*
>
> *Understand that a lot of times when you are dealing with administration, it is kind of a game. You have to know how to play the game, know the rules, and don't get too caught up in it ...don't let it ruin your day. Often, the admin/man-*

agers do things because they lack training, too. They are doing their best with the skills they have. Realize that, and you can help them and get what you want at the same time, instead of blocking them out by saying or thinking, "This is bad," or, "This is dumb."

I found a coach or mentor to be really important as well. I tried to find answers on my own for a long time, and it turned out to be way more difficult. I found it very useful to have a sounding board. The accountability of a coaching call in a couple of weeks forced me to take action and stay in a more proactive stance. That helped a lot.

THE IDEAL JOB MOVE: DR. J

Dr. J was a 34-year-old family doctor who I met while she was on maternity leave for her second child from her small rural practice. She had taken this job position right out of residency because of a desire to "take care of everyone all the time," the gold standard in her residency training. It was just her, another doc and two PAs manning their outpatient practice and the local hospital.

The last straw before reaching out for help had occurred just prior to the start of her maternity leave.

She had been awakened at 2 a.m. to see a patient in the ER and noticed she was growling out a constant stream of profanity as she was getting dressed. She realized if her mother could hear her, she would be ashamed. This was followed quickly by the voice in her head saying, *This is not me. Where is the young idealist who went into med school? When did I become that angry, jaded doctor I swore I would never be?*

Her husband expressed his frustration with the ultimatum that it was time to get a different job or get a different husband—for real.

Dr. J knew she could not go back to the same situation. Her Venn of Happiness overlap was in the 20-30 percent range.

She had to take out some head trash, which told her, "If you leave here, it is because you are a failure. You can't hack it." As if that wasn't enough, her inner critic piled on with, "What if you actually chose the wrong profession, and the next job is even worse?"

Using the Ideal Practice Description, she quickly realized her struggles were built into the practice, and her burnout was not about her as a person or as a physician. She worked for several months on her Master Plan activities, and her Venn of Happiness topped out at 40 percent.

She used her Ideal Practice Description to organize a high quality job search. She created a set of interview questions that transformed her site visits from "I hope they like me" to proving the opportunity would work for her and her family.

She made her move to a full-time family practice position in a larger town and continued to work on her Ideal Practice Description in this new setting. Her IPD overlap here is 80-90 percent, and she feels she can take it even higher.

The tools Dr. J finds most helpful are:

- The Ideal Job Description and Master Plan.
- The Squeegee Breath to reset her energy and let hassles go in her office day.
- BID Huddle and using her whole team, especially her nurse, to address the practice challenges.
- Journaling to process feelings and brainstorm options.
- The book *Transitions* by William Bridges (I provide a copy to all coaching clients).

The one thing she feared about her move to a larger organization was getting lost in the shuffle—a little fish now in a very big pond. In reality, she has moved into a leadership position in the larger group and is in the running to be the medical director of their burnout prevention program.

> *My experience has made me want to help other docs in the same position. I started to talk to others about burnout in general and then slowly about my own struggles. It resonated more than I could have ever imagined. People wanted to talk about this, but they needed someone to step forward and share first.*
>
> *It would be worth it to share that the burnout prevention program we are creating isn't just for my clinic, but for an entire multi-state health system. I'm a little fish reaching a "pond" the size of the Great Lakes!*

Here is just a small piece of Dr. J's advice for other physicians:

> *Don't beat yourself up if every day is not perfect. There is no magic cure for stress. It never goes away—just like diabetics are always having to pay attention to their diet and blood sugar. Stay one step ahead of your practice. If you get behind in your schedule or your charts, it is easy to get stuck in the weeds.*
>
> *Use the Squeegee Breath and BID Huddle to stay on top of things and stay focused. Use your team to share the load.*

Most of all, understand this is not about being a failure …all your colleagues feel the stress, too. We all try to hide it. Don't be afraid to be honest and open up if you are stressed. You will find out we are all feeling the same way. It is really not a competition anymore. We can help each other out. We can all be on the same team.

ON THE LEADERSHIP FAST TRACK: DR. N

When I first met Dr. N, he was practicing part-time in his surgical specialty while holding multiple leadership positions for the hospital, including Chief of Surgery, Head of the Operating Room, and Vice President of the hospital's associated physician group. He felt pulled in multiple different directions and frustrated by the focus on dealing with dissatisfied patients and constantly putting out fires. He wanted to find more time to focus on quality, safety, and mentoring of leaders within the organization.

His job satisfaction was 5 on a 10-point scale. His Ideal Practice was to become the CEO of the hospital, where he intended to make a lasting positive impact and even leave a legacy of quality care—for the patients and staff—at this institution.

One of Dr. N's biggest stressors was the number of meetings he attended each month. He estimated the number at fifteen. When I asked him to list them all, it turned out to be thirty-two. We developed a strategy for handing off those meetings to their rightful leaders. This allowed Dr. N to lead the leaders in brief monthly one-on-one meetings, rather than attend every meeting. He found this to be a huge stress relief, allowing him to focus on proactive work to improve the organization. He was able to take dozens of hours of meeting time off of his monthly schedule.

The tools Dr. N finds most useful are mostly focused on who he is as a leader:

- Pausing for a Squeegee Breath before answering a question or entering a discussion. This is especially helpful if he is experiencing a strong emotion in response to what the other person just said.
- Focusing on listening first. He has started listening for the desires and values behind the words, rather than formulating a response while the other person is speaking. He enjoys using these listening skills to remain connected to his core value that the people are the most important part of any organization.
- Understanding the key distinction of Problem vs. Dilemma. Dr. N has learned how to fix the problems and address the dilemmas with a strategy. He now un-

derstands that the higher up the leadership chain you are, the more likely you are to face dilemmas rather than simple problems. He realizes that a clinician's sense of urgency can be helpful if you need motivation and can cloud your thinking if you are not clear on the ultimate goal.

Dr. N now rates his job satisfaction as 8 out of 10 and is likely to be appointed COO next year and ultimately attain the CEO spot he seeks. His advice for other physician leaders:

> *As a leader, rather than a clinician, it is important to make peace with ambiguity in your life. You won't have all the answers all at once. You have to become comfortable with not knowing what the future entails. It is important to maintain your adaptability and patience with the process of change in the organization, even when you are faced with uncertainty. Focus your attention on being present with your coworkers and direct reports and really listening. Don't allow your assessment of what is not going great to bog you down so much. Focus instead on your vision for what is possible and organizing your people in that direction.*

MAKING THIS PRACTICE THE BEST IT CAN BE: DR. C.

When I met Dr. C., she had just left a very abusive practice situation for a new job with a thirteen provider group in the city. Her overlap with her Ideal Practice Description had gone from 10 percent up to 40 percent with the move, yet she was antsy about this position working out and frustrated by several important factors. These included her new group's culture—no real leadership skills despite being an independent practice in a very competitive market—and her one-hour commute that necessitated her renting an apartment in the city for her call nights.

She concentrated most on who she was being, both at work and at home. She reframed how she viewed her life and stopped focusing so much of her energy on her practice. She built a work-life rebalancing strategy around the answers to the question, "What are the things that are really important to me?"

The tools Dr. C. finds most useful are:

- The "Wheel of Life" (**download your copy in the Power Tools Library at the website**). This tool allowed her to focus her free time on the activities that delivered the most impact on the parts of her life that needed the most attention.

- The Schedule Hack. Dr. C. was actually the co-developer of this technique. It was in working with her that we created and tested the effectiveness of this paper calendar and cell phone life-scheduling process. She does the hack with her family weekly, making sure her distance running workouts, yoga, and alone time with her two children are always included.
- Regular journaling provided a safe place to document her thoughts and feelings. She was able to recognize patterns of thinking (she calls them "mental ruts") that were actually baggage from old job experiences. She was able to see the patterns and change them.
- The Ideal Practice Description **helped her identify the things that worked about this practice and focused on making them even better.**
- The Squeegee Breath. Dr. C. has a unique trigger. When she gets stressed at work, she tends to get impatient with the computer mouse. She will find herself clicking it multiple times until that little spinning ball comes on the screen, and the computer freezes momentarily. The spinning ball is her signal for a Squeegee Breath. She is able to notice and release her impatience, thereby resetting her energy level.

Dr. C. recently adapted the Ideal Practice Description to build an Ideal New Home Description. She used it to key a home search for a move to the city that would end her commute. In a matter of three months, she and her family moved and now live minutes from her practice, within a short jog of the beach. She says this new location is even better than ideal for everyone in the family. (Prior to the move, she was convinced that not only would they never be able to sell their home, but finding a quality replacement in the city would be impossible)

Dr. C's Ideal Practice Description overlap is now 85-90 percent. Her advice is this:

> *You can change anything in the way that you want. You have to be clear on what you want and why you want it—and you have to be willing to be brave enough to take action steps, even if they are baby steps. You can write your IPD down, but you have to be willing to act. Instead of complaining, do something—anything. If you feel stuck, don't be afraid to ask for help—a coach, a physician mentor, a friend. Ask them what is working for them. They will give you a different perspective that is so important.*
>
> *It is possible to be a physician and find balance. It is on a moment-to-moment basis. I talk to myself: "Now I am in the office working" and "Now I am at home*

with my family and am not going to worry about my patients." I focus on what is in front of me at the moment, and that has really helped me compartmentalize.

You can become much better at watching your reactions. "I am angry now... isn't that interesting?" You can learn to stay more grounded in the moment, whether that is in the office, the O.R., or in the midst of a bad delivery. When I say to myself, "I am here now and this is my job in this second," it helps me to not be distracted by all the other things swirling around.

Whatever you do, don't give up on having a balanced life. Figure out what that means to you, and take baby steps in that direction.

A SOLO DOC GOES FROM DOING IT ALL TO CEO: DR. W.

When I met Dr. W, she was an extremely hard working, solo dermatologist seeing forty patients a day, working incredibly long hours, and personally managing a staff of seven people in her practice. She was struggling to maintain any balance in her life. Her two major stressors were the implementation of a new EMR and the day-to-day hassles of managing what she thought were underperforming staff members.

Her Ideal Practice Description overlap was right around 50 percent.

Her action steps to deal with her burnout were nearly all focused on developing leadership skills to share the load with her people.

The tools she feels are most useful are:

- The habit of regularly setting aside time to work on her business, rather than just in it. She found this very useful because of the crush of activities built into any workday in her office practice. Without taking a regular strategic look at her practice and patient flow, nothing was getting better over time.
- Leading by asking questions rather than giving orders. She has found problem solving much easier when she asks her team for help in dealing with their biggest challenges, rather than trying to figure it out all by herself.
- Recognizing the appropriate role for the challenge at hand. Dr. W learned that she wears three "hats" at work—CEO, Dr. W, and Mama W. to her staff, which is all female. She quickly recognized she was being Mama W. much of the time and has learned to operate more frequently from the perspective of the Practice CEO with excellent results.
- Building a schedule that gives her more of the patients she really enjoys. She worked with her staff to build a series of "Quick Look" visits and a "Botox Fast

Lane" mini-clinic into her week for the people who can't wait for her next available appointment (which is always weeks away).

She learned how to run an effective monthly staff meeting and build accountability metrics into all her little improvement projects to keep everyone on track.

Now she still sees forty a day on average, and 85 percent of the time she leaves the office forty-five minutes after the last patient, with all her charts done.

Her Ideal Practice Description overlap is 75–80 percent now.

Dr. W's advice for other physicians:

> *Put your own mask on first. Take the warning signs of burnout seriously, because the negative spiral can affect everything in your life. It is amazing how little changes in my practice made a big difference and put my energy in a very different place.*
>
> *I learned to take responsibility for two things: what is working well AND what is not working. I took responsibility, as the team leader, for the things that were not working well. Then I learned how to help the team address those problems. I didn't have to—and couldn't—do it all myself. I pulled myself back from despairing about getting all the work done. You can too.*

AN ENTREPRENEUR HITS PAY DIRT: DR. C

When I met Dr. C, she was a thirty-nine-year-old primary doctor with a direct pay, cash practice she had been running for seven years. She was struggling to pay the bills, and had taken a part-time medical director position for a weight-loss clinic and a part-time job as a telemedicine contractor to supplement her income.

Her overlap with her Ideal Practice Description was only 30 percent, yet her job satisfaction was 7.5 out of 10. She was not burned out, just frustrated and struggling. Her vision was to build a successful, stand-alone, full-time direct pay practice, and use that success to help other physicians find a pathway out of the rat race to their own cash practice.

Dr. C had no issues with life balance or EMR. Her challenge had its source in the missing skill set all physicians have when they become entrepreneurs—sales and marketing—so we focused almost completely on several core pieces of her marketing plan.

- Visualizing and understanding her Ideal Client
- Learning to speak to that person's issues so they could see the benefits Dr. C could provide rather than just the features of her services
- Creating and selling packages of services rather than charging for visits one at a time

She honed her marketing message and put it out on social media, speaking engagements, the Internet, and even local radio and TV

Dr. C's ideal client is a chronically fatigued, overweight, low-libido, super busy professional woman. She provides them with nutrition and lifestyle coaching, as well as bio-identical hormones as needed. Now she enrolls five-to-seven new patients a week. She has enough volume to take on a nurse practitioner and a pediatrician as employees. She is even opening up a second practice location, something she didn't see as even possible when she started.

She has created a system her employees can use to enroll their own clients, so she can expand the patients the group can see as a whole without Dr. C. personally working harder. Her job satisfaction is a 9 out of 10, despite the fact that her Ideal Practice Overlap is only 50 percent. The reason why? Her newfound success provides her a solid foundation for what she considers to be her "stage two." Once this practice is more delegated and on autopilot, she will begin to give back to her physician brothers and sisters by teaching this alternative practice model.

Dr. C's message for other physicians is:

> *You really can create whatever you want in your life and your practice. It is about knowing what you want to give and finding the people who want to receive that from you. Once you know those two things, find the support people to teach and train and coach you to create your business system.*
>
> *You must think outside your box. Have the courage to reach out for support, and remember to be thankful. Gratitude is very important.*
>
> *I took the dive and committed to making a go of my practice. It was a big move and a point of growth, and completely worth it for all I have developed since then. I even got pregnant along the way (she is due in a month), and my practice now allows me to take off whatever time I want when the baby comes.*

CHAPTER 9

NEXT STEPS

Walking Your Path

"You have brains in your head. You have feet in your shoes. You can steer yourself in any direction you choose. You're on your own, and you know what you know. And you are the person who'll decide where to go."
—Dr. Seuss

"I shall be telling this with a sigh
Somewhere ages and ages hence:
Two roads diverged in a wood, and I—
I took the one less traveled by,
And that has made all the difference."
—Robert Frost

"Nothing in the universe can stop you from letting go and starting over."
—Guy Finley

Burnout's highest and best use is to show you the fork in your road—to point you toward the alternate path that has always been available. Burnout pushes you to live your life more on purpose from this point forward. Burnout done well is a turning point you will look back on and smile about, because this was the time when everything changed for the better. This was when you took the road less traveled by and that made all the difference.

LET'S REVIEW

- I hope you understand burnout now in a whole new way. Perhaps you see it clearly for the first time.
- You can recognize and take out your Head Trash.
- You have the structures to guide your own recovery from burnout and map a path to your Ideal Practice.
  ‣ Your Ideal Practice Description

> ‣ The Venn of Happiness
> ‣ Your Master Plan

- You have learned fifteen field-tested tools to lower your stress and assist you on your journey.
- We have shared leadership tools, so you don't have to work so hard and tools to get more of what you want within a bureaucracy.
- We have talked about the structure of an Ideal Job Search.
- You have gained clarity on your Exit Strategy.
- You have some case study examples of other physician's paths to a more Ideal Practice.

Now it's your turn. Time to take action.

Remember back to the introduction. Recall Einstein's definition of insanity.

"Insanity is doing the same things over and over and expecting a different result."
—Albert Einstein

No matter how much you understand about the concepts contained in this book, nothing will change unless and until you take action.

The only way to obtain *new results* in your life is by taking *new actions*.

This is an authentic opportunity for you to live with purpose. I encourage you to use these tools to build your own Ideal Practice and a rich, juicy, fulfilling life for yourself and your family.

You deserve it.

Now is your time.

One more thing …

Our collaboration does not have to end with the last words of this book.

This can be just the beginning of our work together. I invite you to join a whole community of like-minded physicians and plug yourself into the Power Tools Library at our website.

Use the link below for FREE access to the following nineteen exclusive additional trainings at our support site on the web.

www.thehappymd.com/powertools

ADDITIONAL RESOURCES

19 Power Tools to Stop Physician Burnout

D o not stop here. We have collected all these additional burnout prevention resources (they're free) in the Power Tools Library at our website. Each of these tools expands on what you have learned here in the book to give you deeper levels of stress relieve and connection with your Ideal Practice.

Use this link ***www.thehappymd.com/powertools*** for Instant Access to this exclusive bonus content just for book owners like you.

The Stop Physician Burnout Field Manual

- A printable workbook containing the summaries and action steps from each chapter and section above. It also contains blank documents for your:
  - ‣ Ideal Job Description
  - ‣ Venn of Happiness
  - ‣ Master Plan
  - ‣ Strategy Session Template
- You can download the document to your computer and print off as many copies as you need for as long as you wish into the future.

FREE Discovery Session Consult

My "cup of coffee" conversation to give you a personal strategic plan to end your downward spiral and build your Ideal Practice. You will find a link to schedule this one-hour phone or Skype call with me in the Power Tools Library.

The Burnout Prevention Matrix Report

Contains over 117 ways organizations and physicians can work together to lower stress and prevent burnout.

Physician Burnout Prevention Video Training Series

Short video lessons that reproduce all the sections of chapter one for those of you who learn better from an instructional video.

Satisfaction Mind Flip Report

Mini-training on the Satisfaction Mind Flip technique to focus on what is going right in your life.

Manage Your Boss Worksheet

Full training on how to manage your boss, including the entire question set for your conversations.

Team Huddle Power Training

Video training on the fine points of a well-run BID Team Huddle.

Monthly Team Meeting Training

Video training on how to run an effective Monthly Team Meeting.

Team Problem Solving Protocol

The Team Leader questions to use when your team is solving a problem in your practice.

Universal Upset Person Protocol

Video training on how to deal efficiently, effectively, and empathetically with an upset or angry patient. Perfect to share with your entire team.

Schedule Hack Training

Video training on the Schedule Hack process.

Treat Yourself Like a Dog Video Training

Video training on how to treat yourself like a dog.

What to Do When a Patient Says Thank You Training

How to turn the rare occasion when your patient says thank you into a healing encounter of the highest order—for both of you.

Recommended Reading List

A list of my favorite books on leadership, communication skills, onboarding and more.

Guided Meditation Audio Downloads.

These are downloadable audio files (MP3) with my voice guiding you through a specific imagery experience.

- Body Scan Full Body Relaxation (Head-to-toe full body relaxation for when you want to let it all go).
- Magic Bubble Energetic Boundary Imagery (Learn to maintain your energetic boundaries at work and not be personally drained by patient complaints or suffering).
- Personal Place Relaxation Imagery (A visit to your personal place of healing and rejuvenation. Soak it all up while you are there and come back refreshed and renewed).
- My Day My Way Guided Imagery (A full-body experience of your ideal office day. Helps you experience your Ideal Practice while you are creating it in real life).

Use the following link to plug yourself into all nineteen of these resources in the Power Tools Library at our support website. All of these additional Power Tools are free and my gift to you as an owner of this book: ***www.thehappymd.com/power-tools***.

I wish you all the best in your journey to a more Ideal Practice. If you have any questions, suggestions, or comments about the contents of this book, the Power Tools Library, or your own personal situation, you can reach me at ***www.thehappymd.com/contact***.

Keep breathing, and have a great rest of your day,

Dike Drummond, MD
CEO, *TheHappyMD.com*

ABOUT THE AUTHOR

Dike Drummond, MD is a Mayo-trained family doctor, executive coach, speaker, and consultant on burnout prevention for physicians in all specialties. He is CEO of *TheHappyMD.com*—an online source of tools and information so YOU can be a Happy MD. His online community of over 4000 physicians from 63 different countries has allowed him to create and test the lessons in this book in the real world of practicing doctors and their rapidly changing healthcare environment.

His articles are frequently posted on *KevinMD.com*, *HuffingtonPost.com*, *TheDoctorWeighsIn.com* and other physician-oriented websites.

He has consulted with or been a featured speaker for Kaiser Permanente Northwest, MD Anderson Cancer Center, McKesson US Oncology Network, The Group Practice Improvement Network, the AAFP, the ACPE, the Minnesota Medical Association, and many more.

Dr. Drummond can be reached via this web contact form at *www.TheHappyMD.com/contact* for:

- A free Personal Discovery Session Consult where you will receive an individual strategic plan to recover from burnout and build a more ideal practice
- Inquiries about corporate consulting to implement the Physician Engagement Formula
- Inquiries to arrange live Stop Physician Burnout training for your organization, association, or medical society
- Inquiries for interviews, article reprints, or guest blog posts for your website

ENDNOTES

1. "Enhancing Meaning in Work: A Prescription for Preventing Physician Burnout and Promoting Patient-Centered Care." Tait D. Shanafelt, MD JAMA. 2009; 302 (12):1338-1340.

2. There is very little evidence that Einstein ever said this. Nevertheless, it is absolutely true.

3. "Burnout and satisfaction with work-life balance among U.S. physicians relative to the general US population." Shanafelt TD, et al. Arch Intern Med. 2012 Oct 8; 172 (18):1377-85.

4. Shanafelt TD, West C, Zhao C, et al. "Relationship between increased personal well-being and enhanced empathy among internal medicine residents." J Gen Intern Med 2005; 20:559-64. Firth-Cousins J, Greehhalgh J. "Doctor's perceptions of the links between stress and lowered clinical care." Soc Sci Med 1997; 44: 1017-22. Shanafelt TD, Bradley KA, Wipf JW, Back AL. "Burnout and self-reported patient care in an internal medicine residency program." Ann Intern Med 2002; 136: 358-67. Williams ES, Skinner AC. "Outcomes of physician job satisfaction: a narrative review, implications and directions for future research." Health Care Manage Rev 2003; 28: 119-40. Gardiner M, Sexton R, Durbridge M, Garrard K. "The role of psychological well being in retaining rural practitioners." Aust J Rural Health 2005; 13: 149-55. Wetterneck TB, Linzr M, McMurray J, et al. "Worklife and satisfaction of general Internists." Arch Intern Med 2002; 162: 649-56.

5. "Enhancing Meaning in Work: A Prescription for Preventing Physician Burnout and Promoting Patient-Centered Care." Tait D. Shanafelt, MD JAMA. 2009; 302 (12):1338-1340.

6. "Development of burnout over time and the causal order of the three dimensions of burnout among male and female GPs. A three-wave panel study." I. Houkes, et al. BMC Public Health. 2011; 11: 240

7. These tools are the basis of the Organizational Development philosophy of "Appre-

ciative Inquiry" and the parenting philosophy of "Catch your kids doing something right." Also, see the questions in the book *First Break all the Rules* referenced below. Most of all though, try these tools out in your own life and see what changes.

8. *First Break All the Rules*. Buckingham M. Coffman C. Simon & Shuster, 1999.
9. Better!
10. *Nurture Shock*. Bronson P. Merryman A. Twelve Publishers, 2011.
11. *First Break All the Rules*. Buckingham M. Coffman C. Simon & Shuster, 1999.

CPSIA information can be obtained at www.ICGtesting.com
Printed in the USA
LVOW02s0606261114

415618LV00002B/7/P